D1220629

Frank Lloyd Wright's Dana House

DONALD HOFFMANN

DOVER PUBLICATIONS, INC.
Mineola, New York

NA
7238
.S65
H64
1996

To the memory of
George C. Hoffmann and Ines Catron Hoffmann

VISITING THE HOUSE

The Dana house stands at Fourth Street and Lawrence Avenue in Springfield, Illinois. It was purchased in 1981 by the state of Illinois and is now operated by the Illinois Historic Preservation Agency as a house museum. For tour hours and information call 217/782-6776.

Copyright

Copyright © 1996 by Donald Hoffmann.
All rights reserved under Pan American and International Copyright Conventions.

Published in Canada by General Publishing Company, Ltd., 30 Lesmill Road, Don Mills, Toronto, Ontario.

Published in the United Kingdom by Constable and Company, Ltd., 3 The Lanchesters, 162–164 Fulham Palace Road, London W6 9ER.

Bibliographical Note

Frank Lloyd Wright's Dana House is a new work, first published by Dover Publications, Inc., in 1996.

Library of Congress Cataloging-in-Publication Data

Hoffmann, Donald.
Frank Lloyd Wright's Dana House / Donald Hoffmann.
p. cm.
Includes bibliographical references and index.
ISBN 0-486-29120-0 (pbk.)
1. Dana House (Springfield, Ill.) 2. Prairie school (Architecture)—Illinois—Springfield. 3. Wright, Frank Lloyd, 1867–1959—Criticism and interpretation. 4. Springfield (Ill.)—Buildings, structures, etc. I. Title.
NA7238.S65H64 1996 96-4804
728.8'092—dc20 CIP

Manufactured in the United States of America
Dover Publications, Inc., 31 East 2nd Street, Mineola, N.Y. 11501

LONGWOOD COLLEGE LIBRARY
FARMVILLE, VIRGINIA 23901

Acknowledgments

ANY STUDY OF the Dana house enjoys several advantages. The house itself survives, carefully restored and lovingly maintained. Earlier studies, especially those conducted for the state of Illinois, identify many obscure sources. The archives at the house, moreover, are close to other research centers, and to walk to the Lincoln Library or the Illinois State Historical Library is to traverse the very ground that once knew Lincoln's footsteps. All of which is not to say that the building can be quickly fathomed as a work of art; the house has been at the back of my mind for more than fifty years.

For making the house and archives available on so many occasions and for discussing many details, I am particularly indebted to Donald P. Hallmark, the site manager since 1981. Rick La Follette, assistant site manager, and Chris Bastin and Kathy Liesman, site technicians, graciously offered their help, as did Cindy Levin, executive director of the Dana-Thomas House Foundation. Visits to the Sangamon Valley Collection at the Lincoln Library were always a pleasure because of the courteous and efficient staff: Edward J. Russo, city historian and author of *Prairie of Promise: Springfield and Sangamon County*, Melinda Garvert and Curtis Mann. At the Illinois State Historical Library, now a division of the Illinois Historic Preservation Agency, Thomas F. Schwartz, state historian, kindly helped me with several questions about Lincoln. Mary Michals, curator of the audio-visual collection, and E. Cheryl Schnirring, cu- ... s, also provided help. Tom Wood of the Illinois Regional Archives Depository at Sangamon State University kindly retrieved old county records.

Among those who so generously answered my queries are Terrence L. Marvel at the Prairie Archives of the Milwaukee Art Museum; Mary Jane Hamilton, an independent scholar; Shonnie Finnegan, university archivist for the State University of New York at Buffalo; Bill O'Malley, architecture bibliographer at the Avery Library of Columbia University; and Marianne A. Kane of the Greene County Public Library, Xenia, Ohio. This study also drew on the resources of the Getty Center for the History of Art and the Humanities, Santa Monica, California; the Burnham Library at the Art Institute of Chicago; the Kansas City Public Library; the library of the Nelson-Atkins Museum of Art, Kansas City; the Nichols Library at the University of Missouri–Kansas City; the Murphy Library at the University of Kansas, Lawrence; and the Chicago Public Library.

For their great help in furnishing illustrations, I thank Bruce Brooks Pfeiffer and Oscar Muñoz of the Frank Lloyd Wright Archives at Taliesin West, Scottsdale, Arizona; Wilbert R. Hasbrouck of Chicago; Janet Parks and Dan Kany of the Avery Library at Columbia University; Eileen Sullivan at the Metropolitan Museum of Art; L. E. James Helyar, curator of graphics in the department of special collections, the Spencer Library at the University of Kansas; Nancy A. McClelland of Christie's, New York; Julia Meech and Mosette Broderick of New York; Meg

LONGWOOD LIBRARY
1000297793

Klinkow, director of the research center at the Frank Lloyd Wright Home and Studio in Oak Park, Illinois; Mrs. Henry Carawan of Los Angeles; Jennifer Watts at the Huntington, San Marino, California; Robert T. Cozzolino at the Art Institute of Chicago; and particularly Doug Carr of Springfield, Illinois, whose fresh photographs of the house are without equal.

An account of the Dana house titled *Bannerstone House*, by Tom R. Cavanaugh and Payne E. L. Thomas, was published in 1970. The acquisition of the house in 1981 by the state of Illinois led to more detailed studies. Those undertaken by what was then the division of historic sites in the Illinois Department of Conservation included "Susan Lawrence," by Richard S. Taylor, and "Frank Lloyd Wright's Downstate Illinois Prairie House: the Evolution of Springfield's Dana-Thomas House," by John Patterson, both dated 1982. Taylor was also instrumental in securing for the Illinois State Historical Library the important Earl R. Bice collection of the Susan Lawrence Dana family papers. *Frank Lloyd Wright and Susan Lawrence Dana*, published by Sangamon State University in 1985, offered essays by Taylor on "Susan Lawrence Dana, Feminist" and by Mark Heyman, a former Taliesin apprentice, on "Wright and Dana: Architect and Client." Also helpful were the "Revised Dana-Thomas House Restoration Report and Summary" of 1991–92, by the Illinois Historic Preservation Agency, and two other publications of 1992, *Frank Lloyd Wright's Dana-Thomas House*, by Donald P. Hallmark, and *The Dana-Thomas House, Springfield, Illinois, Fact Book & Tour Guide*, by David Diederich.

For their encouragement, I thank Mark Heyman, W. Philip Cotton, Jr., Pamela Kingsbury and George Hoffmann, John Hoffmann and Fred Hoffmann, my brothers. And for their care and collaboration in so many projects, I am grateful to the officers and editors of Dover Publications, Inc.: Hayward Cirker, Clarence Strowbridge, Stanley Appelbaum and James Spero. "God save us all from architectural historians," Wright used to tell his assistants; one can only hope that he left room for exceptions.

D.H.

Contents

List of Illustrations

Frank Lloyd Wright's
Dana House

1. *Susan Lawrence Dana house, east front.*

2. *Dana house, looking northwest.*

The Site and the Times

IN 1900, THE year he turned 33, Frank Lloyd Wright at last began to find his voice. Not long after, in Springfield, Illinois, he seized the chance to test his entire range [Figs. 1, 2]. The house of 1902–04 for Susan Lawrence Dana, a woman of means, became the largest house Wright had built, the most ornamental, the most vital in its contest between mass and space. It also became the most paradoxical.

Comprehensive and complex, the Dana house stretched along its site to evoke the romance of the frontier and the freedom of the vanished prairie [3]. But it was crowded by the railroad at its back and by the state capitol and center of town nearby [4]. The long horizontal also collided indoors with spaces two stories tall, where the sense of the open landscape gave way to a world more like a child's dream, with steps everywhere up and down, overlooks and covert

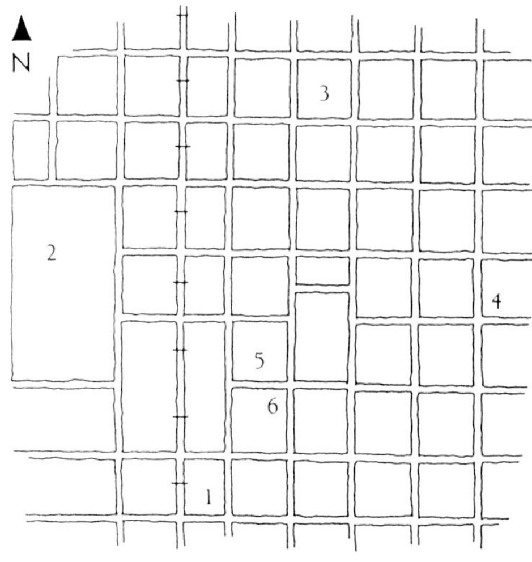

4. *Center of Springfield, Ill.: (1) Dana house; (2) state capitol; (3) courthouse and square; (4) home of Abraham Lincoln; (5) governor's mansion; (6) home of Vachel Lindsay.*

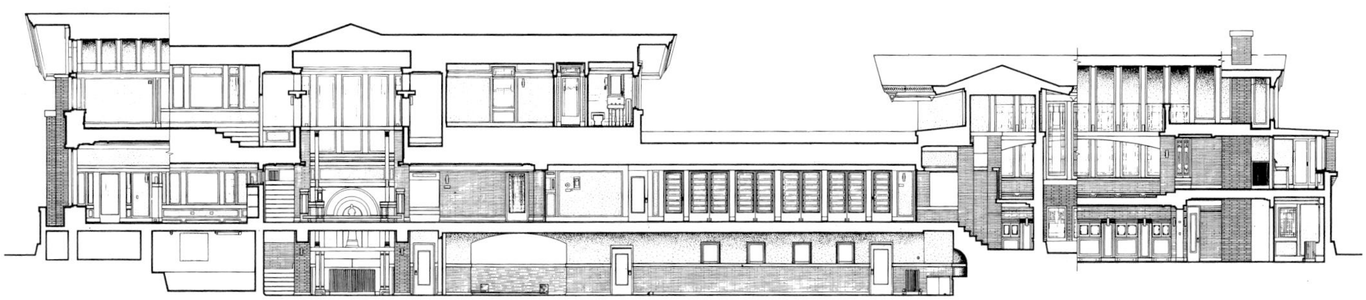

3. *Longitudinal section, looking south.*

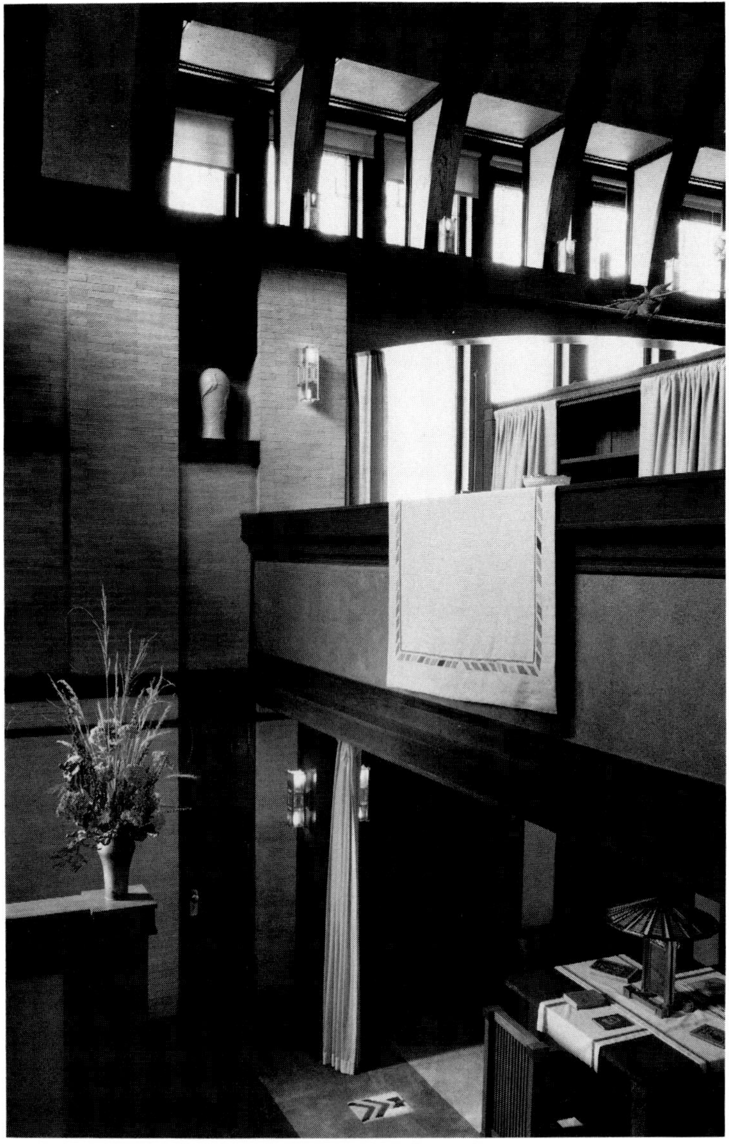

5. *Vista toward library, below, and studio; looking predominantly south.*

nooks, softly colored lamps and sudden vistas toward partly hidden places [5]. Through such episodes of space and light, the interior unfolded slowly, to a more Victorian rhythm, and its visual grammar grew intricate and various. Glass patterns conceived purely as geometric inventions kept company with others abstracted from plants and even insects. Allegorical sculptures led to a room with landscape murals of unembarrassed realism.

So far as the principles of architectural structure, or what John Ruskin declared the three good architectures of the world, the house expressed all three at once, thus invited tensions and ambiguities not easily resolved. The principle of the gable, so vigorously asserted by the roofs, perforce contended with that of the post and lintel, but also with the arch and the vault, which lingered from the years Wright had spent as a draftsman for Adler & Sullivan. The house at the same time took strength from dynamic principles of structure far beyond architectural tradition.

Here was Frank Lloyd Wright at full tilt; but surely the house meant something else to Mrs. Dana. Why would a widowed woman without children build a place of such size and splendor? And why next to a railroad? For her, the house must have risen as a grand affirmation in the wake of staggering personal losses: not only a new residence, but a beacon of culture and high society, as well as a memorial to the man whose money built it, R. D. Lawrence, her father [6].

Rheuna Drake Lawrence, who sometimes spelled his surname "Lawrance," possessed the uncommon ability to succeed at any number of enterprises, public or private. He could not be counted among the earliest settlers of Springfield, but his years there reached back to the time of Abraham Lincoln, whom he may well have known; the presence of Lincoln strangely permeated the town. Early in 1859 the elder sister of Lawrence's wife married a young lawyer with political ambitions, Charles S. Zane, who soon was pleased to be in Lincoln's company on May 18, 1860, at the moment Lincoln first learned of his nom-

6. *R. D. Lawrence.*

ination to the Presidency. When he departed for the White House on February 11, 1861, Lincoln left behind his law partner, William H. Herndon, and Herndon chose Zane to be his new partner. Then, too, in a note of January 1864 to Edwin M. Stanton, the Secretary of War, Lincoln wrote, "If another Assistant Quarter-Master is needed to serve in Central Illinois, or with Illinois troops, let Mr. Lawrence be appointed."[1]

Lawrence, much like Lincoln, witnessed the great changes of the time and the steady transformation of his town. The quaint means of travel and transportation afford a brief but telling index. Lincoln came to Illinois in 1830 by wagon and ox team, and first saw Springfield a year later by taking a large canoe down the Sangamon River and hiking more than five miles into town. In 1837 he moved there with all he owned on the back of a borrowed horse. After 24 years he left town for the Presidency from the depot of the Great Western Railroad. The building arts in Springfield had progressed still more swiftly. The town was founded somewhat artificially, but decisively, with a stake driven into the prairie some 600 feet above sea level; the stake signified the temporary seat of Sangamon County. The first courthouse, a log cabin that cost $72.50 to build, was twice succeeded within a decade, first by a frame building and then by one of bricks. At the boom time of the mid-1850s, when Lawrence chose Springfield as a good place to be a bricklayer, the town claimed seven brickyards and an annual output of six million bricks. Small wonder that he would someday build a home of bricks, and so would his daughter.[2]

Life was short, and Lawrence was quick to learn about building. His mother, Susan Minerva Lawrence, born in 1813, was already a widow when she married Lewis W. Lawrence in 1836, and she became a widow again when her second husband died of pneumonia in April 1849. He had served in the Mexican War of 1846–48. Their son Rheuna, born January 18, 1837 at the farm home near Cedarville, Ohio, proved dutiful yet precociously independent; he may have left home at ten. In any event, he went to work in a brickyard, to bear off the fresh-made bricks, and at 14 earned journeyman's wages as a bricklayer. He pursued his trade in Fort Wayne, Indiana, and then in Chicago, where he became a foreman. To his mother he sent the larger part of his pay. Around 1856 he moved to Springfield, where, before he reached his majority, he became a building contractor. He first built a three-story structure downtown, at Fifth and Jefferson Streets. In 1857, with a partner, he built the Universalist Church at the northwest corner of Fifth and Cook Streets, two blocks from the corner where he would one day build his home. But his first great success, also in 1857, was to win the masonry contract for six buildings and additions at the Illinois State Hospital for the Insane, in Jacksonville. There exists a frail copy of the *Daily Illinois State Register* for June 18, 1857, which he kept all his life, announcing that bids were due July 1. The work took several years, and it entailed some three million bricks and three thousand perches of stone.[3]

When he married Mary Agnes Maxcy on January 24, 1859, Lawrence was 22 and his bride a few weeks shy of 18. They soon took Lawrence's mother into the household; she stayed until her death in 1892. Their first child, born in November 1859, was named Agnes Salome Lawrence, but she lived less than a year. A second daughter was born October 13, 1862.

[1]A memo on the envelope identified the subject as R. D. Lawrence; see *The Collected Works of Abraham Lincoln*, ed. Roy P. Basler (New Brunswick, N.J., 1953), vol. III, p. 141. Herndon recalled that Lincoln wanted the Lincoln & Herndon shingle to stay at the entrance to their office, then on the west side of the square, and said, "If I live I'm coming back some time, and then we'll go right on practising law as if nothing had ever happened." See William H. Herndon and J. W. Weik, *Herndon's Lincoln* (Chicago, 1890), vol. III, pp. 482–484. Also see David Donald, *Lincoln's Herndon* (New York, 1948), pp. 157, 247. In June 1862, Herndon represented Lawrence in a legal matter. For the career of Zane (1831–1915), see J. C. Power, *History of the Early Settlers of Sangamon County, Illinois* (Springfield, Ill., 1876), pp. 796–797; *History of Sangamon County, Illinois* (Chicago, 1881), p. 120; *The Bench and Bar of Illinois*, ed. J. M. Palmer (Chicago, 1899), pp. 193–94; Historical Encyclopedia of Illinois, ed. Newton Bateman and Paul Selby (Chicago, 1908), vol. 1, p. 604; Emanuel Hertz, *The Hidden Lincoln* (New York, 1938), pp. 377–379, and the *Illinois State Journal*, March 30, 1915, p. 11. His wife, the former Margaret D. Maxcy, died in 1912.

[2]Founded in 1821, Springfield briefly was renamed "Calhoun" in 1823; see *The Edwards Papers*, ed. E. B. Washburne (Chicago, 1884), p. 211. Although it is often said that "Sangamon" derived from an Indian word signifying the land of plenty, Virgil T. Vogel writes in *Indian Place Names in Illinois* (Springfield, Ill., 1963), pp. 123–125, that in fact it refers to the "river mouth" or confluence with the Illinois River a few miles north of Beardstown. Also see *The Collected Works of Abraham Lincoln*, vol. IV, p. 65; *History of Sangamon County, Illinois*, p. 555; J. C. Power, *History of Springfield, Illinois* (Springfield, Ill., 1871), pp. 11–12; and Paul M. Angle, *"Here I Have Lived": A History of Lincoln's Springfield 1821–1865* (Springfield, Ill., 1935), pp. 6, 26, 43, 169.

[3]The construction project in Jacksonville, 35 miles west of Springfield, may explain why Lawrence does not appear in a Springfield city directory until 1859. Vital records in Greene County, Ohio, do not date earlier than 1869; the best data are in the Bice Collection of Susan Lawrence Dana family papers in the Illinois State Historical Library, Springfield. Profiles of Lawrence appear in the *History of Sangamon County, Illinois*, p. 687; *Encyclopaedia of Biography of Illinois* (Chicago, 1902), vol. III, pp. 12–17; and Joseph Wallace, *Past and Present of the City of Springfield and Sangamon County Illinois* (Chicago, 1904), vol. II, pp. 1411–1414.

They named her Sue C. Lawrence, but because the initial stood for nothing else, "Sue C." easily evolved into "Susie." In the years to come, through caprice or marriage, her name changed five more times. Susie Lawrence would learn that nothing about life was certain, and certainly not life itself.[4]

R. D. Lawrence thrived during the years of the Civil War. In 1868 he spent $6000 for a prominent homesite only two blocks from the governor's mansion. The corner site, where a friend of Lincoln's had once lived, was in that central part of town where the street grid tilted two degrees east of due north. Lawrence bought two lots for an 80-foot front on Fourth Street and two more lots for an equal front on Third. The alley between the two pairs of lots had been vacated in 1863. That gave the property a fine reach of 241 feet along the street named Wright—not, of course, for Frank Lloyd Wright, but for the educator, surveyor and fervent abolitionist Erastus Wright, who arrived in Springfield in 1821 and later claimed to have built the first frame house there in 1823. In August 1833 he surveyed into town lots a 60-acre tract that had been sold earlier in the year for only $300. In 1842 a cabinetmaker named Daniel Ruckel, who knew Lincoln, bought the lots that later became the east part of the Lawrence homestead. Ruckel built a small house, expanded his property in 1850, and in August 1851 mortgaged it to Lincoln for a loan of $300. Lincoln charged ten percent a year, then a modest rate of interest. "Daniel E. Ruckel," he wrote much later, "was a dear friend of mine; and any favor done a member of his family would be appreciated by me."[5]

Ruckel died in 1854 at only 42, but he had lived long enough to see the railroad, known most often as the Chicago & Alton, come along Third Street at the west edge of his property. The depot stood at Third and Jefferson Streets, only a block east from where the town was founded, and on May 3, 1865 it became the last stop for Lincoln's funeral train. Lincoln had understood what railroads meant. In March 1832, in his first published message to voters, he hailed them as a "never failing source of communication." It was six years before the first locomotive appeared in Illinois on order from the Northern Cross, conceived to link the central prairies to the Illinois River, which in turn flowed into the Mississippi and toward large markets. Then more of the prairie soil might be profitably tilled. A steamboat carried the first locomotive to Meredosia, and the Northern Cross finally reached Springfield in 1842. It failed very soon. Revived a few years later, it eventually became part of the Great Western, which ran along Tenth Street on the east side of town. Ice on the Illinois River, however, could still halt commerce. The town of Alton, situated on the Mississippi north of St. Louis, promised Springfield a less seasonal port. In 1851, Lincoln represented the Alton & Sangamon Railroad Company in pursuing shareholders delinquent in paying their installments. He himself owned six shares. This was the road that would begin to run along Third Street in 1852:

> The first train of cars from Alton came into the city on Thursday afternoon [September 9], about five o'clock. Their approach was announced by the firing of cannon, and the train was received by a national salute and the cheers of the citizens present. The cars immediately returned. Arrangements will now be made for running the cars regularly—and the hour for arrival and departure will soon be announced.[6]

The fact that trains rattled by the Lawrence homestead signaled a victory for the west side of town: not so much a nuisance as an amenity. After the war, Lawrence himself ventured into railroad contracting—"150,000 Cross Ties Wanted on the Line of Gilman, Clinton and Springfield Rail Road," he advertised in undertaking to build a road that would

---

[4]The office of the Sangamon County Clerk has no birth records prior to 1877; again, the Bice Collection is the best source. Besides a family birth record, it includes a bank account from 1870 and a numerology card.

[5]Letter of March 13, 1862, in which Lincoln recommends Curtis H. Hall, a son-in-law of Ruckel, for a post at the New York Customs House; see *The Collected Works of Abraham Lincoln*, vol. V, p. 157. For the loan to Ruckel, ibid., vol. II, pp. 109, 201, 422. Lincoln knew Ruckel (1811–1854) as early as 1839; See Harry E. Pratt, *Lincoln 1809–1839* (Springfield, Ill., 1941), p. 191. An 1854 survey map of Springfield shows Ruckel's house at the corner. Lincoln's house stood seven blocks away, at the northeast corner of Eighth and Jackson Streets. Also see the "Abstract of Title" in the Dana house archives. Lawrence bought lots 7–10 of Block 3, W. H. Allen's Addition, on Jan. 24, 1868.

[6]*Illinois Daily Journal*, Sept. 11, 1852, p. 3. It was identified as the Alton & Sangamon railroad, although three days later an advertisement of departure times called it the Alton & Springfield. In later years it was variously called the St. Louis, Alton & Chicago; the Chicago & St. Louis; and the Chicago, Alton & St. Louis. In 1832, at only 23, Lincoln ran unsuccessfully for the Illinois legislature. Although he praised railroads, he favored improvements to the Sangamon River to make it navigable; see *The Collected Works of Abraham Lincoln*, vol. I, p. 5; also vol. II, p. 98 and vol. IV, p. 189. Also see Power, *History of Springfield, Illinois*, p. 32. By the end of 1852 there were 412 miles of operating railroads in Illinois. Four years later, there were 2135 miles. By 1925, Springfield had 139 main line crossings at grade, and between 1908 and 1922, 35 persons were killed at grade crossings of the Chicago & Alton; see M. H. West et al., City Plan of the City of Springfield, Illinois (Chicago, 1925), p. 48.

7. *R. D. Lawrence house, looking northwest.*

reach 111 miles north and later become part of the Illinois Central. If the Italianate villa he built at Fourth and Wright Streets failed to find a place among the 67 prominent residences cited by J. C. Power in his 1871 *History of Springfield, Illinois,* it nonetheless stood as an impressive residence for a young man who had come to town as a bricklayer [7].

In 1872, with three partners, Lawrence sank a coal-mine shaft and laid out the company town of Barclay, 11 miles northeast of his home and conveniently next to the new Gilman, Clinton and Springfield line. He managed the company for seven years. Today the mine is gone, and Barclay survives as little more than a signpost; but two of Lawrence's commercial buildings in downtown Springfield stand as testimony to his pride in masonry construction. He built the Central Block in 1881 at the southeast corner of Sixth and Adams Streets and immediately leased it to the John Bressmer Company, the leading dry-goods store [8]. (Bressmer, a German who arrived in Springfield

8. *Central Block, southeast corner of Sixth and Adams Sts.*

9. *Lawrence Building, 227 South Sixth St.*

10. *Susie Lawrence Dana, in Minneapolis.*

in 1848 at the age of 15, first went to work on the street in front of Lincoln's home; he saw Lincoln come and go, but lacked sufficient English to speak with him.) Not far south on Sixth Street, the asymmetrical front of the Lawrence Building betrayed a remodeling of two older fronts [9]. Here, by 1880, Lawrence had his offices. But he must have built the new front in a later year.[7]

On the occasion of Susie Lawrence's marriage, on December 4, 1883, it was reported that after her debut in society she had "easily maintained the position she at once took as one of the reigning belles."[8] She looked much like her father, yet the lesson he must have intended by giving her a savings account at only seven evidently had gone unlearned. Edwin Ward Dana, the man she married, had grown up about 30 miles away in Lincoln, Illinois, where his father ran the abstract and title office. His family came from the same New England tree that bore the brilliant but erratic Charles A. Dana, once an Assistant Secretary of War under Lincoln and later the editor of the New York *Sun*. Edwin Dana and Susie Lawrence settled in Minneapolis, where he dealt in real estate [10].

R. D. Lawrence kept busy as ever. In later years he gained even greater prominence.[9] He served as

---

[7]A deed of March 2, 1881, shows that Lawrence paid $23,500 for the property that measured 47 feet on Sixth St. and 110 feet on Adams, once the site of the American House, the town's leading hotel. The second site has a 36-foot front and a depth of 70 feet. Bressmer's career is outlined in *Portrait and Biographical Album of Sangamon County, Illinois* (Chicago, 1891), pp. 201–202.

[8]*Illinois State Register*, Dec. 5, 1883, p. 3.

[9]Lawrence was an early benefactor of the Springfield Home for the Friendless, and a volunteer firefighter from 1864 to 1869—thus exempted from poll tax, highway and street labor, jury duty and military service. In 1877 he was appointed by the governor to the commission for building the Southern Illinois Penitentiary. He was president of the Springfield Board of Trade in 1881, and in 1884 became a commissioner for the completion of the new state capitol.

mayor from 1891 to 1893, then joined the board of education and later became its president. He was also president of the reorganized State National Bank, at the southwest corner of the courthouse square. He had invested in mines in Leadville, Colorado, and in Josephine County, Oregon. Despite the silver panic of 1893 his monthly ledgers from Leadville showed dividends as high as $36,000. Lawrence was a wealthy man.

Dana did not fare so well, either in business or in marriage. Occasionally he borrowed money from his father-in-law. In 1893, the year of the World's Columbian Exposition, he grandly identified himself as president of the Western Business Agency in Chicago, with branch offices in nine other cities. But by 1894 the company had disappeared, and Dana and his wife were living back where they had been married, in the Lawrence home. Dana went to work for his father-in-law and eventually managed the mines in Oregon. One mine failed and he started to work another, near Leland, with only primitive equipment. His wife stayed at Grants Pass, about sixteen miles away. "I hope you may soon have a barrel full of gold and then come home and be happy," her father wrote her on August 17, 1900, "or come home and be happy without the barrel."[10]

She soon came home, but with the body of her husband. Dana had been hoisting ore on September 2, a Sunday afternoon, when a harness snapped, causing the sweep of the capstan to spin in reverse, strike him in the chest and kill him. Death had already taken their two infant sons, and a few months later, on February 17, 1901, death came to the mainstay of the family, R. D. Lawrence.[11]

---

[10]Letter in the Bice Collection. "I get nothing but bad news from Leadville," Lawrence had written his daughter a year earlier. "I wish Ed could make a grand strike out there [in Oregon]." The collection agency in Chicago listed S. L. Dana as its treasurer; see the Chicago City Directory for 1893, p. 1722.

[11]For the death of Dana, see the *Lincoln Daily Courier*, Sept. 3, 1900, p. 4 and Sept. 4, 1900, p. 6; and the *Illinois State Register*, Sept. 4, 1900, p. 6. The infant sons were Lawrence Henry Dana, who was born Dec. 10, 1885, and died the same day, and Edwin Whitney Dana, born Aug. 22, 1887, who died Oct. 5, 1887. For obituaries of R. D. Lawrence, see the *Illinois State Register*, Feb. 18, 1901, p. 1; the *Illinois State Journal*, Feb. 18, 1901, p. 6; and the *Springfield News*, Feb. 18, 1901, p. 1.

Circumstances, Plans and Construction

THE DEATH OF R. D. Lawrence, mourned though it was, left Mrs. Dana free to live and build on a lavish scale. She began her new life by taking a most dubious route to her inheritance. For his part, Frank Lloyd Wright rarely ignored an opportunity, and when it came to spending someone else's money, he hardly stood on principle. The probate record tells almost nothing about the Lawrence estate or its true value. Mrs. Dana in fact withdrew her father's will, and to keep its contents as unknown as the extent of his wealth, she presided over its disappearance. Many years later she scribbled a few sentences to clear the air; but even the conservator of her own estate grew convinced that she had conspired to circumvent her father's wishes.

Three weeks after her father died, Mrs. Dana deposited his will with the county court. A notice of March 20, 1901 in the *Illinois State Journal* listed nine legatees. But the ostensible witnesses to the will, two officers of the State National Bank, said it was not signed in their presence. Judge G. W. Murray—in 1884 he had been the last law partner of William H. Herndon, the last law partner of Lincoln—refused the will for probate. He named Mrs. Dana administrator on April 17, and on May 8 granted her an extraordinary privilege. She could withdraw the will if she preserved it for future use in court. She did not.[1]

Almost a year later, on April 14, 1902, Mrs. Dana filed an inventory and appraisal that merely listed eight parcels of real estate with no declared value and other assets described only as sundry notes, stocks, bonds and cash totaling $70,125. Expenses came to more than $11,000. From the balance she distributed $19,684.93 to her mother and $39,369.85 to herself. A note found among her effects appears to be an aide-mémoire for J. F. Bunn, cashier of the State National Bank and one of the nominal witnesses to her father's will. It may offer a clue to the cost of the new house. Dated to the time of Lawrence's final illness, the note says to "put aside about ninety thousand dollars paper for Susie in case of death." Thus it is possible Mrs. Dana had spoken with her father about extensive improvements to the homestead. For

[1]See the Rheuna D. Lawrence probate file no. 5700, microfilm P473, Sangamon County Circuit Court. George W. Murray (1839–1926) in 1920 recalled of Herndon: "Continuously, when we were not busy, and perhaps at some times when we should have been at work, he talked to me of Lincoln"; see William E. Barton, *The Paternity of Abraham Lincoln* (New York, 1920), p. 363. For an obituary of Murray, see the *Illinois State Journal*, March 18, 1926, p. 1.

a building program of any great scope she needed more than a regular income from rents and dividends.[2]

People would talk, especially in a town the size of Springfield. As the new house was being finished, Mrs. Dana, too, worried about the way she had handled the estate. She continued to worry for years to come. "There can be no confusion after I am gone," she wrote as though beginning an *apologia pro vita sua* in September 1926. The will was rejected on a mere technicality, she wrote, and she was appointed administrator at her mother's request. They decided to honor all bequests as if the will had been valid, and to prove they acted in good faith they kept receipts for the payments. The largest, $5000 in cash and $5000 in municipal railroad bonds, went to Flora Lawrence, an unmarried cousin of R. D. Lawrence's who had lived since 1872 in his home.

None of those distributions, however, was recorded by the court. The probate record ended as mysteriously as it began; in August 1931 the sheriff's department reported that Mrs. Dana could not be found in Sangamon County, thus could not be served with a summons to show cause why she had not produced her father's will. Long afterward, the conservator of her estate said R. D. Lawrence had left his fortune in trusts for his wife and daughter, but Mrs. Dana conspired to withdraw the will, an act contrary to law, to gain immediate access to his wealth.[3]

How much could Wright have known? He recalled many years later that in 1902 Mrs. Dana already donated the art and science wing of the Hillside Home School, a building he designed for his aunts near Spring Green, Wisconsin, and lent $27,000 to complete the main block. The house she planned to build in Springfield, moreover, called for large resources. Other facts hint at a sly complicity. Wright titled the drawings for the new house "Alterations and Additions, Dwelling of Mrs. R. D. Lawrence": a double deception, given that the house would in fact replace the Italianate villa and would serve primarily Mrs. Dana, not her mother. Then, too, the drawings showed the centerline for the new construction as coincident with that of the old villa—again as if the program amounted to a remodeling. In his autobiography, finally, Wright hardly mentioned the house, then barely hinted at what had happened:

> The Dana House at Springfield—dear old Mother Lawrence—salt-risen bread, blackberry preserves, and the way we kept faith with the old homestead.[4]

Life in the Italianate villa after the death of R. D. Lawrence found Mrs. Dana at the center of a household of women: her mother, her grandmother Farnetta Maxcy, who very soon died in August 1902, and cousin Flora Lawrence. Could a new and stylish residence give the survivors some measure of happiness and stability? Then as now, residents of Springfield in search of culture looked first to Chicago. Springfield by 1900 was still a small town of 34,000 people. Chicago boasted a population 50 times that number; it had the Art Institute, a symphony orchestra, an academy of sciences and a young university already known for its extraordinary faculty. Wright, too, was making his mark. Shortly after he left Adler & Sullivan he exhibited his own projects in the Chicago Architectural Club annuals of 1894 and 1895, at the Art Institute. Pictures of his modest home in Oak Park appeared in one of the first issues of *The House Beautiful*, in February 1897. That winter he collaborated with W. H. Winslow, his first major client, to produce a private edition of William C. Gannett's essay by the same title. (Of the ninety copies, Mrs. Dana came to own the eighty-seventh, doubtless a gift from Wright. She also placed a photograph of Wright in her new living hall.) *The House Beautiful* was still being published in Chicago when it presented Wright's home again, now with the studio addition, in December 1899. The commentary was by the architect Alfred H. Granger:

> I have called Mr. Wright a radical opponent of ancient styles. While he carries his opposition to antiquity to a far greater extent than many of us can agree with, it is refreshing to come into contact with a genius so fresh, so truthful and so full of vitality . . . .[5]

[2]The note by Bunn is in the Bice Collection; so is a receipt that shows Mrs. Dana in May 1902 paid an Illinois inheritance tax of only $665.79, which, with the $20,000 exemption, indicates an estate of $86,579. On the basis of known costs for other Wright houses of those years, Donald P. Hallmark, the site manager, estimates the cost of the Dana house at $60,000.

[3]Conversation with Earl R. Bice, Sept. 4, 1964. J. W. Templeman, a lawyer, petitioned the probate court on Aug. 5, 1931 to examine the Lawrence will; presumably he represented relatives of Lawrence.

[4]*Frank Lloyd Wright: Collected Writings*, ed. B. B. Pfeiffer, vol. 2 (New York, 1992), p. 289. Wright mentions the funding of the Hillside Home School in a revised edition of *An Autobiography* (New York, 1943), p. 383.

[5]"An Architect's Studio," *The House Beautiful* VII (Dec. 1899), pp. 44–45. Mrs. Dana's copy of the Gannett book is listed in her estate, Record book 47, Inventory no. 5908, pp. 465–466, in the Illinois Regional Archives Depository at Sangamon State University, Springfield.

In the spring of 1900, at the thirteenth Chicago Architectural Club annual, Wright exhibited a profusion of views of his Oak Park studio and its furnishings, and in June that year the *Architectural Review* of Boston published the first thorough account of his architecture. His friend Robert C. Spencer, Jr., explained the work accurately and described Wright as "a leader of revolt against dead custom."[6] In 1901, in the February issue of *The Ladies' Home Journal*, Wright published his prototype design for "A Home in a Prairie Town." It was the very month when R. D. Lawrence died. On March 6, in a spirited lecture at Hull-House, Wright denounced "the utter helplessness of old forms to satisfy new conditions" and praised the artist "who accepts, works, and sings as he works, with the joy of the *here* and *now*."[7]

But if it was in 1902 that she approached Wright, and after the Lawrence estate had been settled, Mrs. Dana may have been inspired by a visit to the Art Institute. In March, at the fifteenth Chicago Architectural Club annual, Wright mounted a dazzling display of his art—in all, 65 exhibits. (It was enough to impel the young Barry Byrne, who for ten years had dreamed of becoming an architect, to seek an interview in Oak Park and a place in Wright's studio, both of which he got.) The skills Wright exercised in publicizing his own work, however, paled by comparison to his powers of self-presentation, so remarkably effective even in the world of business. A letter that William E. Martin wrote to his brother in October 1902 bears witness:

> I have been—seen—talked to, admired, one of nature's *noblemen*—Frank Lloyd Wright . . . . A splendid type of manhood . . . he is *pure gold*.[8]

To the prospect of designing a house, Wright brought a particularly high sense of purpose. In 1896 he declared himself the chosen interpreter of the individuality of his clients, with an "opportunity to characterize men and women in enduring building material for their betterment and the edification of their kind."[9] The old hierarchy of building types, he said, did not hold true in America; the home environment had a far more intimate influence on spiritual growth and physical well-being than the cathedral or palace. By the time of the Dana house, Wright could pronounce the construction of a residence singularly important:

> . . . no opportunity seems to me quite so much THE opportunity of one's life as the building of the home unless it is the choosing of one's wife or one's husband, as the case may be.[10]

His studio in Oak Park had become a floating world like that of the Japanese woodblock prints he so admired. The staff ebbed and flowed according to the amount of work to be done; usually, his assistants numbered around six. Their loyalty proved exceptional, given the fact that Wright remained so cavalier about paying them on time, if at all. They came to the studio to take part in a new and vital architecture. Wright said he felt a message burning within him. He relished his chance:

> . . . to make of a building, together with its equipment, appurtenances and environment, an entity which shall constitute a complete work of art . . . sure to be uplifting and helpful in the same sense that pure air to breathe is better than air poisoned with noxious gases.[11]

Like the waste of a million seeds for a single new plant, he wrote, it might take a million buildings for only one small instance of genuine architecture. His work demanded an "unrelenting concentration, giv-

[6]"The Work of Frank Lloyd Wright," the *Architectural Review* VII (June 1900), p. 72.

[7]Wright, "The Art and Craft of the Machine," in *Catalogue of the Fourteenth Annual Exhibition of the Chicago Architectural Club* (Chicago, 1901), n.p. The Chicago Arts and Crafts Society had been formed at Hull-House on Oct. 22, 1897, and the crafts shop there was directed by several residents who were members of the society, Jane Addams writes in *Twenty Years at Hull-House* (New York, 1910), p. 375. "What a fine possession she has been for Chicago," Wright said of Miss Addams in 1918; see *Frank Lloyd Wright: Collected Writings*, vol. 1 (New York, 1992), p. 158. Garry Wills, in "Sons and Daughters of Chicago," the *New York Review*, June 9, 1994, p. 58, calls Miss Addams "the greatest single figure in the city's history—not only the city's conscience, but its needed support in crisis after crisis." It is not known when Mrs. Dana first met Miss Addams, or whether Miss Addams brought Wright to her attention.

[8]Jack Quinan, *Frank Lloyd Wright's Larkin Building* (New York, 1987), pp. 4–5. W. E. Martin and his brother Darwin D. Martin both became clients of Wright's. For the career of Barry Byrne (1883–1967), see Sally Kitt Chappell and Ann Van Zanten, *Barry Byrne, John Lloyd Wright: Architecture & Design* (Chicago, 1982) and H. Allen Brooks, *The Prairie School* (Toronto, 1972).

[9]*Frank Lloyd Wright: Collected Writings*, vol. 1, p. 29.

[10]Wright, letter of March 27, 1903 to Darwin D. Martin, University Archives, State University of New York at Buffalo.

[11]Wright, "In the Cause of Architecture," the *Architectural Record XXIII* (March 1908), pp. 162–163. Also see *ibid.*, p. 156.

ing up the best and deepest in me to an ideal I loved better than myself."[12]

Barry Byrne remembered the studio as having a certain magic. The assistants benefited largely from an aura. Wright needed helpers, but by temperament and choice he could not pretend to be a teacher. As an artist and individualist, he demanded complete control:

> . . . even to the size and shape of the pieces of glass in the windows, the arrangement and profile of the most insignificant of the architectural members.[13]

Or, as he wrote in his autobiography:

> The system, or lack of it—I have never had an office in the conventional sense—has become fixed habit, and works well enough because I stay directly with it in every detail . . .. Where I am, there my office is. My office is "me."[14]

Characteristic of the Oak Park studio was the youth of everyone there; toward the end of 1902, when Wright was 35, the key assistants were Marion Mahony, 31, and Walter Burley Griffin, William E. Drummond and Andrew Willatzen, all 26. Barry Byrne would turn 19 a few days before Christmas. None of the assistants could match Wright's sense of scale and proportions, the intensity of his effort to achieve right relationships, the sheer exuberance of his imagination. In writing of his own partnership in 1913, George Grant Elmslie, who sometimes had helped out at the studio, said "we can't *touch* him, and never will."[15] Much later, Byrne would recall:

> Wright seldom worked on an idea without making it almost transcendentally [sic] better. The value of training under Wright lay in the matter of seeing top grade talent, or shall I say genius, function. There was no one around him that in any way approached him in ability.[16]

The program Mrs. Dana brought to the Oak Park studio can be deduced from the house itself and from the description Wright provided of the "city dwelling for Mrs. Susan L. Dana" in the portfolio of drawings he published in Berlin in 1911 [11]. (She began the formal use of "Susan" in 1903, and by 1911 there was no reason to pretend that the house was built for her mother, who had died in 1905.) Wright's words:

> A home designed to accommodate the art collection of its owner and for entertaining extensively, somewhat elaborately worked out in detail.
>
> Fixtures and furnishings designed with the furniture.
>
> It is not entirely new. The old house, which was incorporated in the structure, is outlined by a heavy line on the plan.
>
> The gallery [the studio] is designed as a gathering place for the artistic activities of the community, and to accommodate the collection made by its owner.

[12]*Frank Lloyd Wright: Collected Writings*, vol. 2, pp. 91, 219.

[13]Wright, "In the Cause of Architecture," p. 164.

[14]*Frank Lloyd Wright: Collected Writings*, vol. 2, p. 278. Wright's lack of regard for his assistants may have been inspired by Louis H. Sullivan: ". . . he would often say to me with undisguised contempt: 'Wright! I have no respect at all for a draftsman!'"; see *Genius and the Mobocracy* (New York, 1949), p. 41.

[15]Elmslie (1868–1952) met Wright about 1887 in the office of J. L. Silsbee, where they both worked. He considered Sullivan and Wright "very great men," but judged Wright "the greater, by far, in the art of expression." See Craig Zabel, "George Grant Elmslie and the Glory and Burden of the Sullivan Legacy," in *The Midwest in American Architecture*, ed. John S. Garner (Urbana, Ill., 1991), p. 23.

[16]Letter of May 3, 1951 quoted in Mark L. Peisch, *The Chicago School of Architecture* (New York, 1964), p. 45.

11. *Dana house, south front, rendering of 1910.*

> It is connected by a covered passage with the house, the passage itself serving as a conservatory.
>
> The hall, dining-room and gallery extend through two stories, and with the ceilings formed in the roof.
>
> The terra cotta figure at the entrance was modeled by Richard W. Bock, sculptor.
>
> The interior walls are of cream-colored brick closely laid. The woodwork is of freely marked red oak.
>
> The sand-finished plaster ceilings are ribbed with wood and stained. Around the dining-room is a decoration of sumac (the plant motif for the decoration of the house proper) and fall flowers, stained in the sand-finished background by George Niedecken.
>
> The furniture and fittings were designed with the buildings.[17]

The site of course came first. Lawrence had enlarged it, but also cluttered it with additions, outbuildings and even another house—a cottage into which his wife's parents soon moved. In 1893 and 1894, through a series of purchases and title conveyances, he broadened the frontage on Fourth Street from 80 to 109.66 feet, and on Third Street from 80 to 105.65 feet. The unequal dimensions and slight tilt of the north property line resulted from an old and slanted quarter-section line. Only one other house stood on the rest of the block. It belonged to Stuart Brown, who in 1886 had joined his father's law office—which could trace its history to Brown's grandfather, John Todd Stuart, the man who encouraged Lincoln to study law and took him as a partner from 1837 to 1841.[18]

The original Italianate villa, foursquare and compact, measured only about 30 by 34 feet. Most of the additions were recorded on an 1896 fire-insurance map [12]. It showed the cottage at the southwest corner of the site, the carriage house to the north and two attachments to the villa itself. The first, a story-and-a-half tall, evidently was built as a summer kitchen. The two-story addition that linked it to the main house afforded a larger dining room for Lawrence's extended family, a space that indeed would establish the width of the dining room for the new house. In August 1900, Lawrence began to build a brick washhouse and stable. The washhouse, he wrote his daughter in Oregon, "suits your Mama muchly."

So far as the site itself, the salient feature remained the grand exposure to the south, a sweep of 241 feet. (By 1890 the street had been renamed Douglas Avenue, and in 1898 it became Lawrence Avenue. It was paved with bricks, like Fourth Street. The streets of Springfield notoriously went unpaved until 1878, when cedar blocks were introduced. Bricks were first used in 1888.) Wright envisioned a house facing south, spread along Lawrence Avenue and yet fully respectful of Fourth Street. As constructed, the building enclosed about 9200 square feet on the first and second stories and afforded more than 1700 square feet of finished space in the basement. It extended 169 feet and, together with the walled garden court, decisively controlled its site [13]. Wright clearly meant to shape and define as much space as he could.[19]

[17] *Ausgeführte Bauten und Entwürfe von Frank Lloyd Wright* (Berlin, 1911), caption to plate XXXI.

[18] The city directory shows that Brown (1860–1924) was living just north of Lawrence's house by 1887. He had married in 1886. Also see Paul M. Angle, *One Hundred Years of Law* (Springfield, Ill., 1928).

[19] Ward W. Willits, after studying the plan for his house in Highland Park, Ill., wrote Wright on May 4, 1902 that he doubted "the wisdom of so great a width overall on a 200-foot lot. Better narrow it down some so we will have more lawn"; see Mark David Linch, "The Ward Willits House by Frank Lloyd Wright," in the *Frank Lloyd Wright Newsletter*, vol. 2, no. 3 (1979), p. 1. For the paving of Springfield's streets, see *The Illinois Capital Illustrated* (Springfield, Ill., 1898), p. 39.

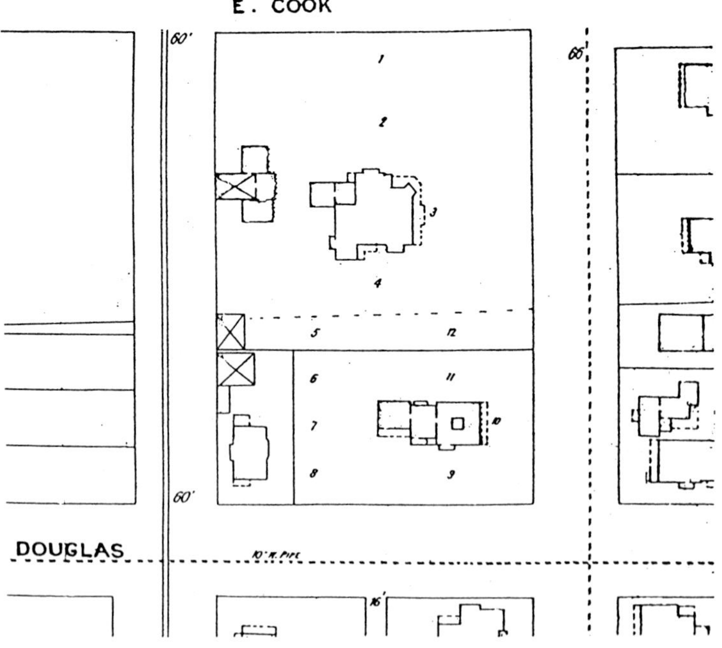

12. *Map of 1896; Lawrence house and cottage on lots 6–11, Stuart Brown house to the north.*

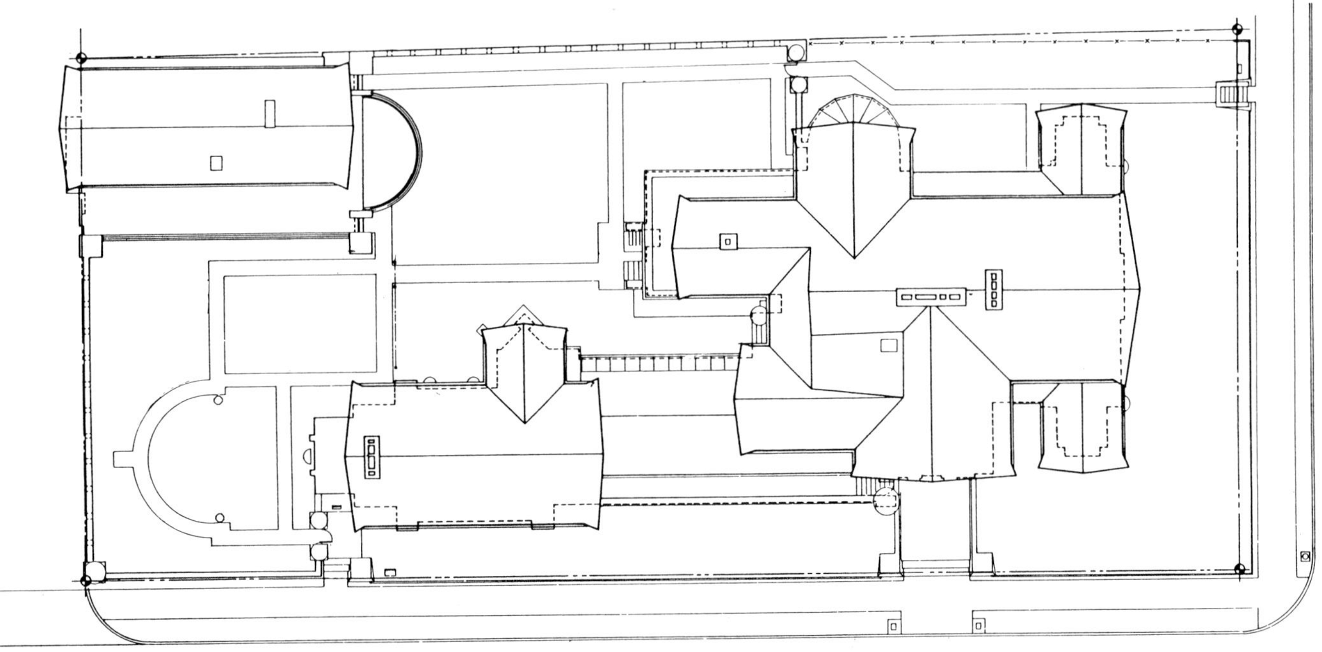

13. *Site plan, Dana house, garden court and carriage house.*

Conception and composition, he said at Hull-House, transformed an original impulse, perhaps registered unconsciously, into an organically consistent entity. The ground plan presented "only a purposeful record of that dream which saw the destined building living in its appointed place," he wrote later:

> A good plan is the beginning and the end, because every good plan is organic. . . . There is more beauty in a fine ground plan than in almost any of its ultimate consequences. In itself it will have the rhythms, masses and proportions of a good decoration if it is the organic plan for an organic building with individual style—consistent with materials.[20]

Brick, an inherently architectural material, lent itself nicely to the articulation of a plan. The articulate plan—mature in the relation of its parts, rhythmic and even syncopated—found a parallel, he continued, in the music of Bach [14]. Accentuated piers and condensed masonry masses composed a pattern that could flower through the ornamental details of the building. As the record of a dream, the plan be-

[20]Wright, "In the Cause of Architecture: The Logic of the Plan," the *Architectural Record LXIII* (Jan. 1928), p. 149.

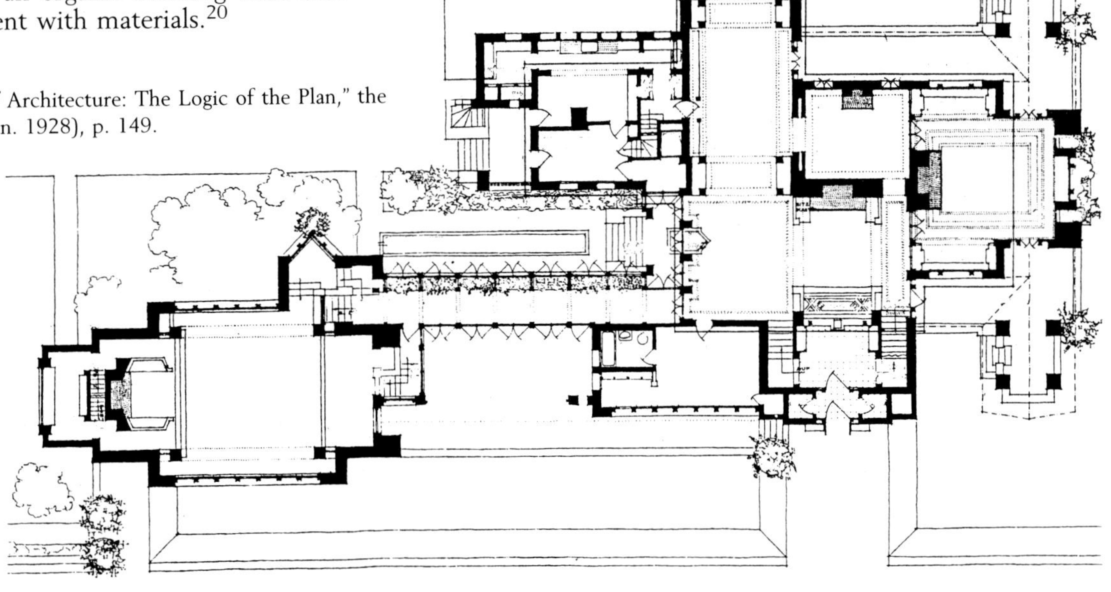

14. *First-floor plan as redrawn for publication in Berlin.*

Site work began in the summer of 1902, long before the working drawings were revised, and so far as the public knew, the building project simply involved changes to the old villa:

> Excavations have been completed at the Lawrence home and work of remodeling the home of the widow of the former president of the Springfield board of education soon will be well under way. An entirely new roof of tile will be one of the many improvements.[23]

Wright gloried in his large capacity for self-review and his equally severe discipline in bringing embryonic ideas toward the full bloom of maturity. Thus the revised working drawings, dated January 18, 1903, show a vast improvement [19–24]. And other revisions are still to come.

First, the house has grown larger; the kitchen reaches farther north, the verandas expand into corner pavilions, a polygonal bay sprouts from the dining room. A bowling alley appears in the basement, below the long corridor to the studio. Glass prisms in the south terrace can cast sunlight into a room probably intended for billiards. A few walls survive from the old house and help to shape and determine the size of the new rooms. But when he wrote in 1911 that the villa had been "incorporated in the structure" of the new house, Wright chose his words carefully; almost nothing from the villa remains visible. The living hall, dining room, kitchen and living room exceed the old boundaries, and the rest of the new house extends beyond the perimeter of the villa and its additions. The metamorphosis is as complete as that of a caterpillar turned into a butterfly.

[23] *Springfield Sunday Journal*, Sept. 14, 1902, p. 4. Mrs. Dana, her mother and cousin Flora Lawrence moved temporarily to 225 E. Lawrence Ave. while the new house was in construction. The building permit and early assessment records have not survived.

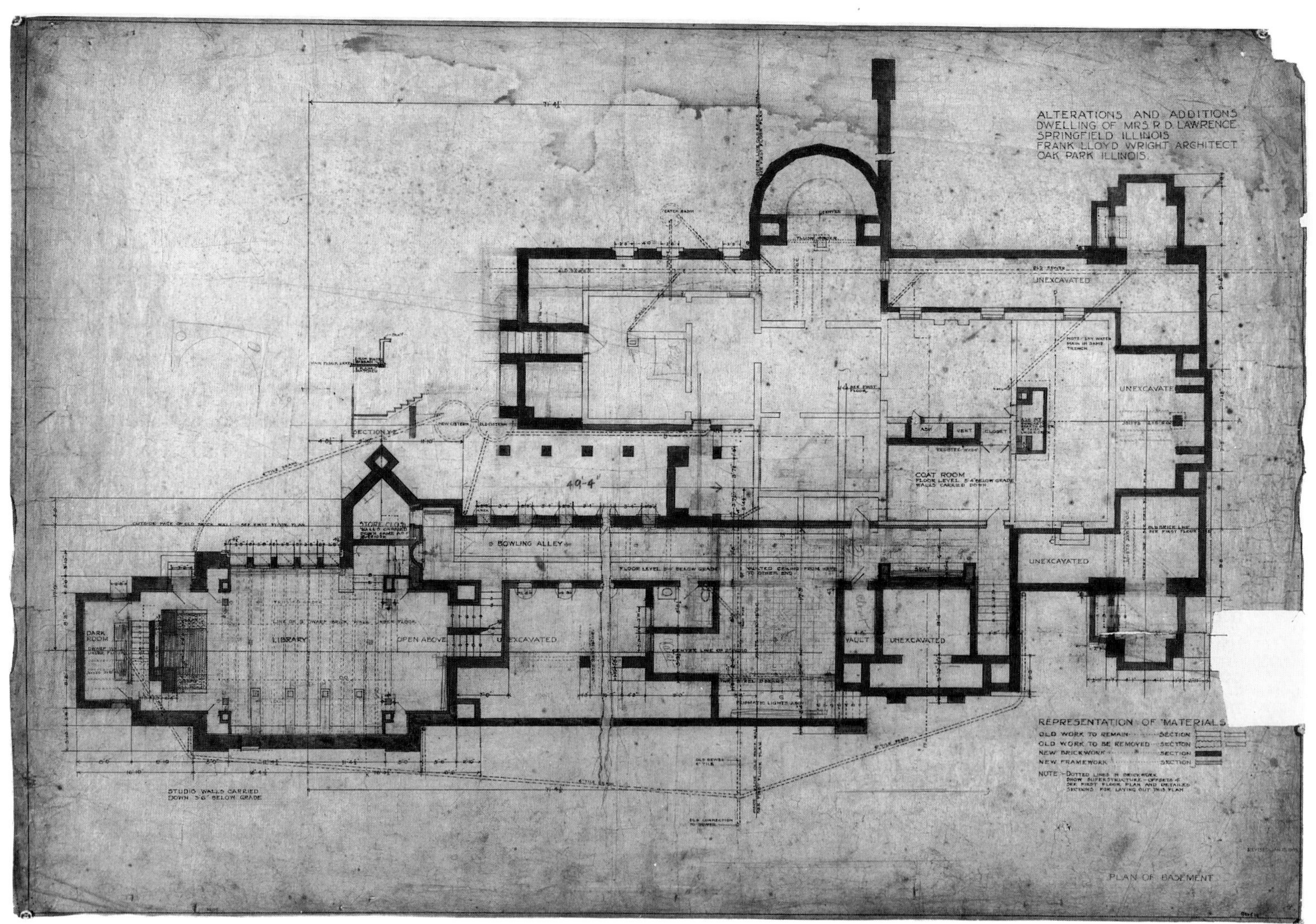

19. *Revised basement plan.*

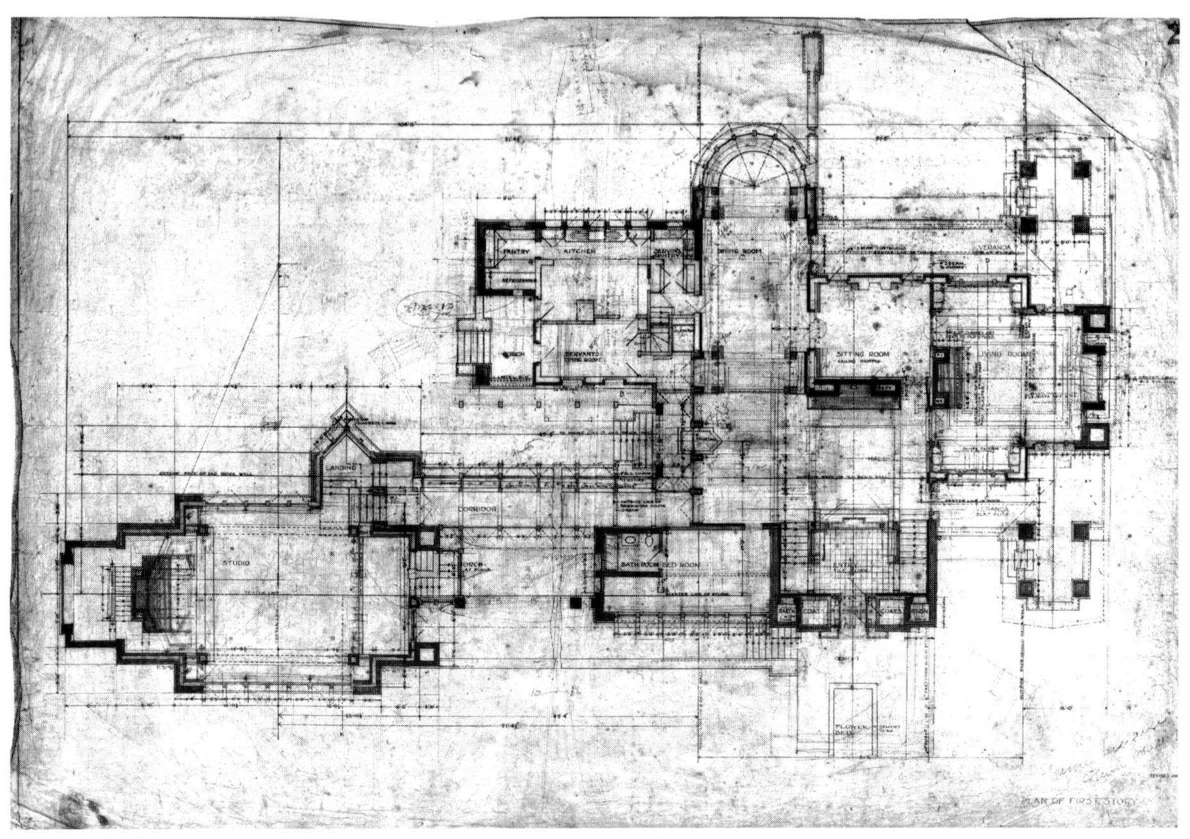

20. *Revised first-floor plan.*

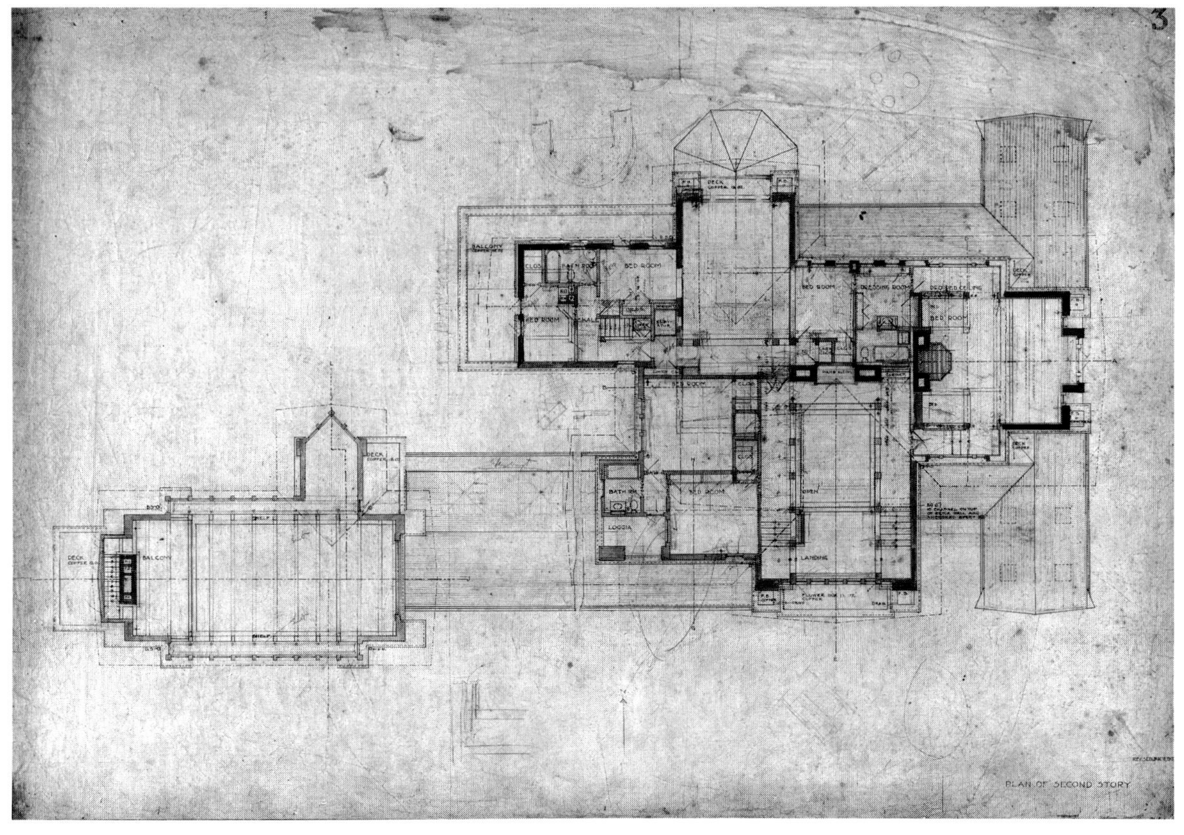

21. *Revised second-floor plan.*

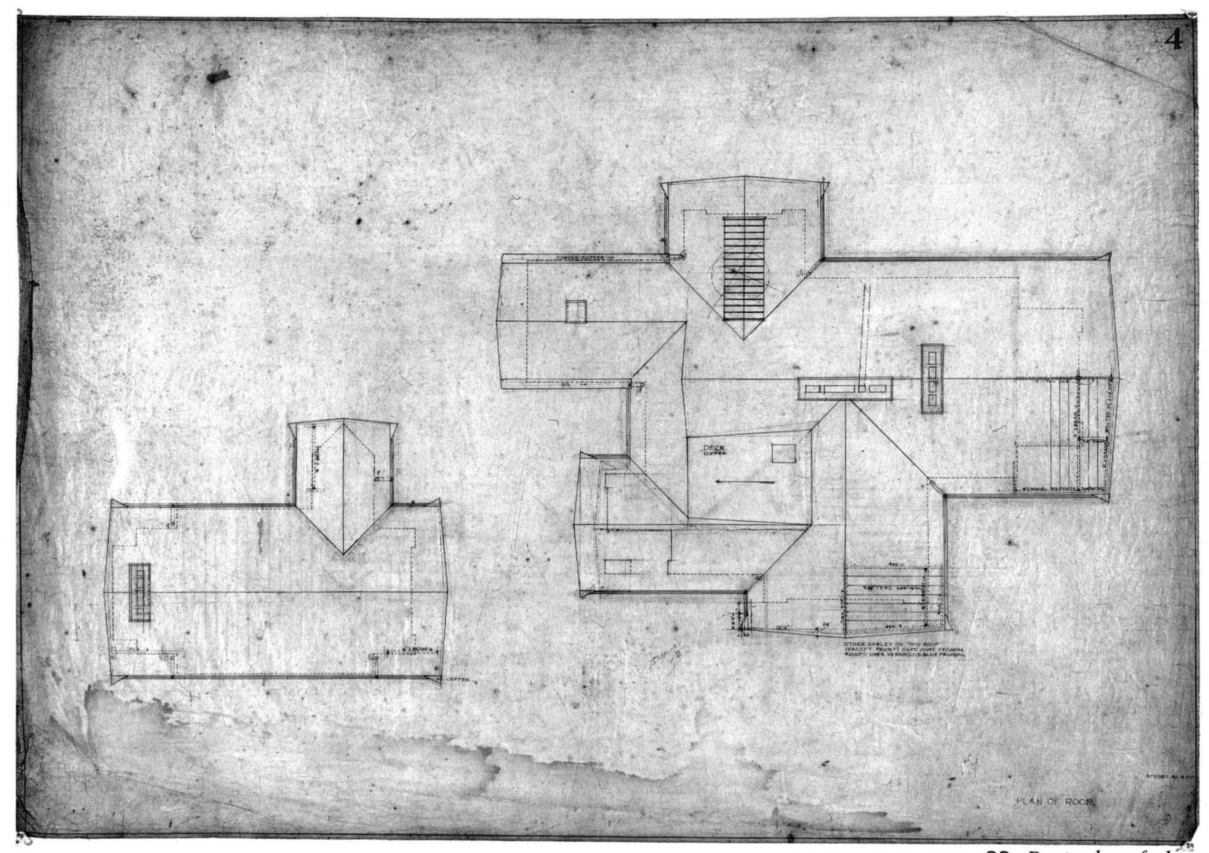

22. *Revised roof plan.*

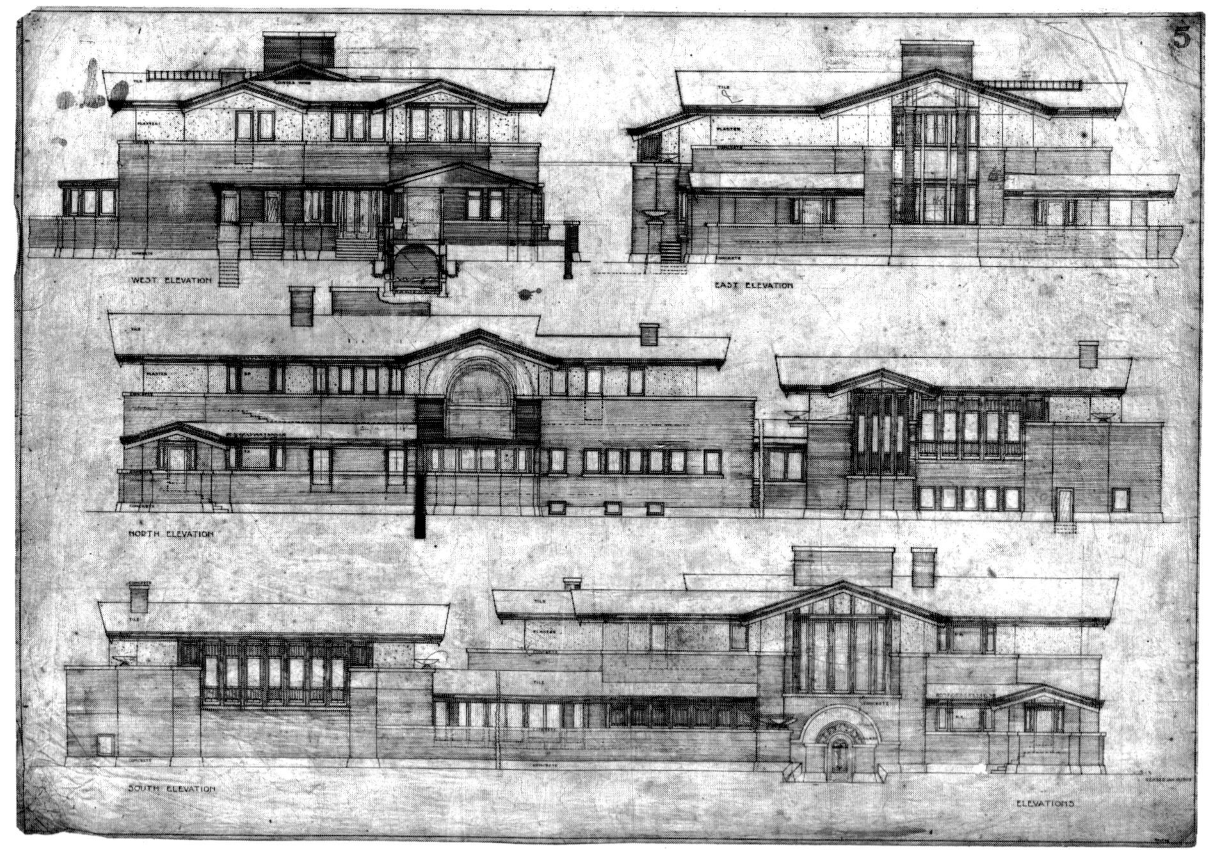

23. *Revised elevations.*

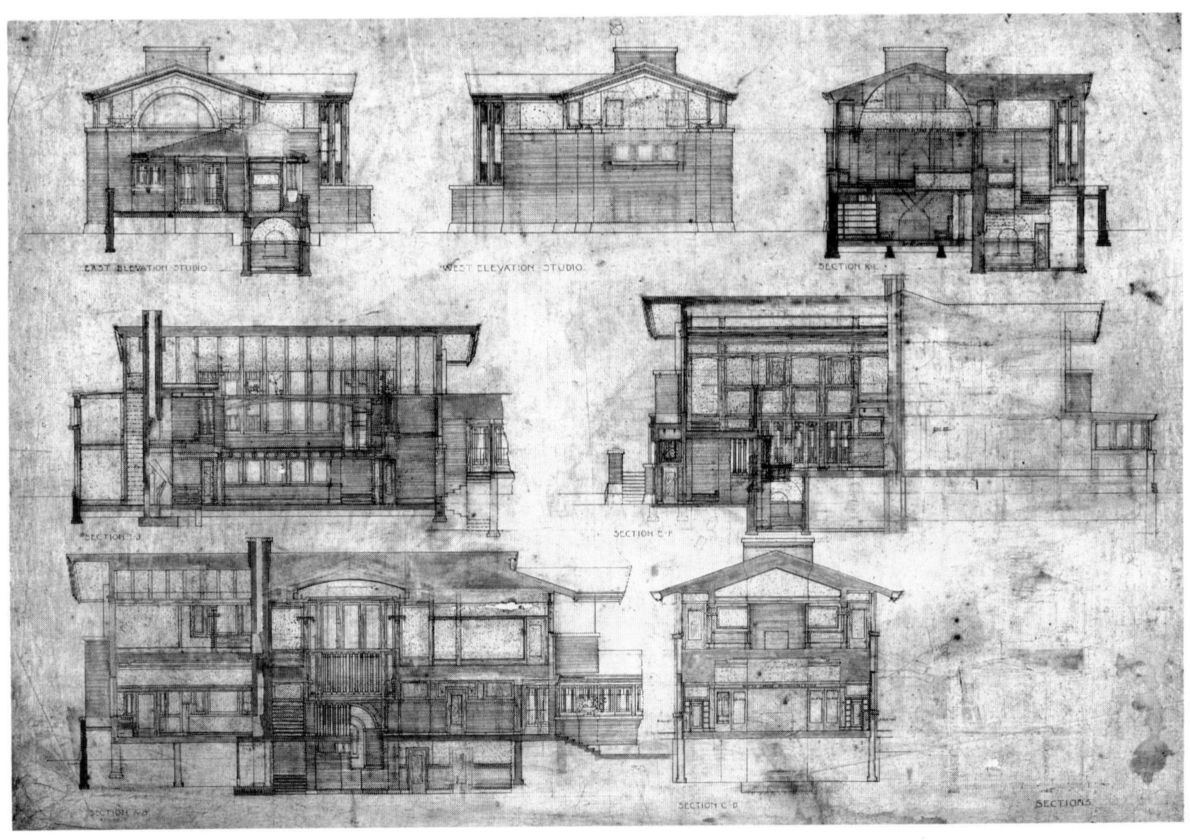

24. *Revised elevations and sections.*

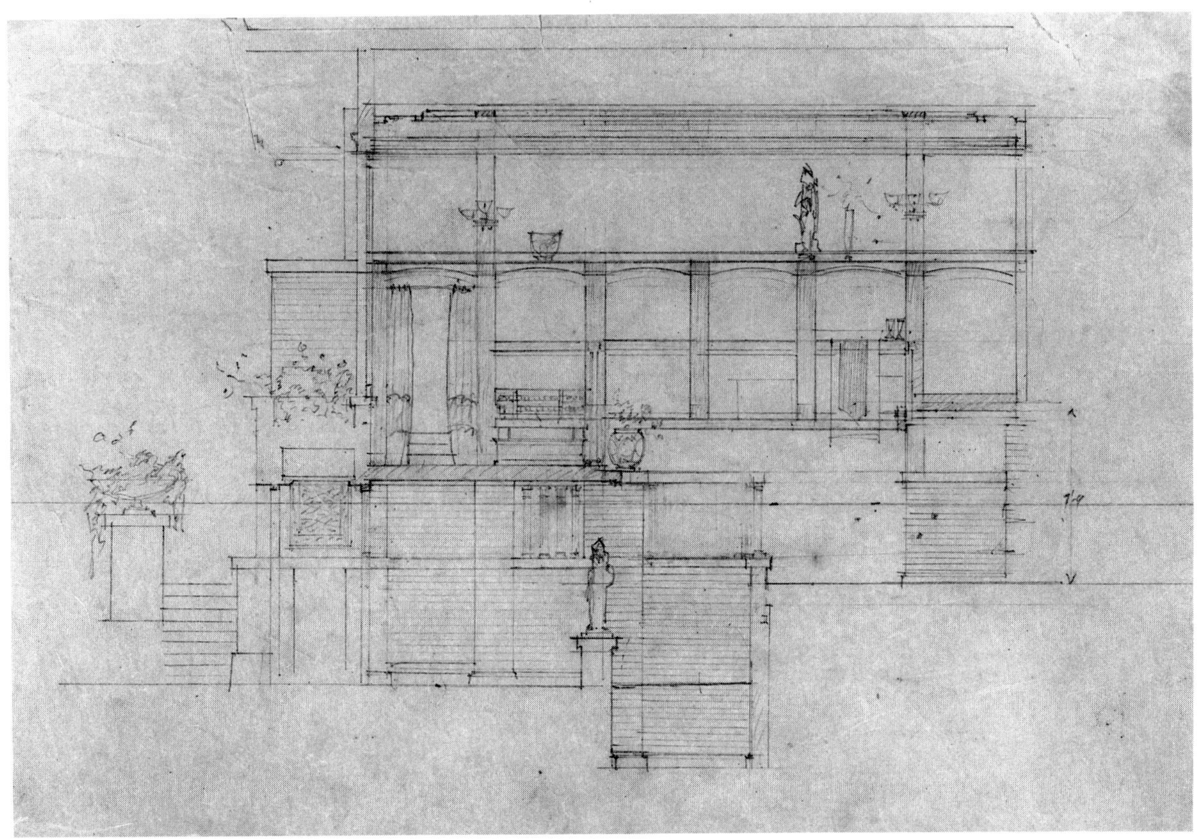

25. *Study for living hall.*

With two decisive strokes, Wright made sense of the first-floor plan and managed to hide the sitting-room fireplace, the last remnant of the Italianate villa. He consigned to the basement all that had obstructed the central space: the vault, toilet room, coatroom and niche. And he turned the living hall south, onto axis with the vestibule and entry. Now the heart of the house became a space about 36 feet square, the northeast quarter taken by the sitting room and the entire south half by the living hall. The westward reach of the hall could give easily to all the other social spaces—the dining room, garden court and studio [25].

The zigzag path from the entry through the hall and into the dining room resembles the plan of a house Wright designed much earlier for George Blossom, in Chicago [26].[24] But as a major destination for large social events, the dining room of the Dana house now rises two stories to a ribbed and vaulted ceiling, and in effect becomes a dining hall [27]. A change in the kitchen shifts the servants' dining room to the south side of the service wing; the northwest corner of the wing becomes instead a pantry and refrigerator room. The quarters for Mrs. Lawrence are better developed as a suite with a dressing alcove as well as bathroom. On the second floor, the rooms for cousin Flora Lawrence are also improved, so as to share a bathroom and the small loggia, and across the court the balcony for the servants' bedrooms is extended along the north side of the house.

26. *George Blossom house, first-floor plan.*

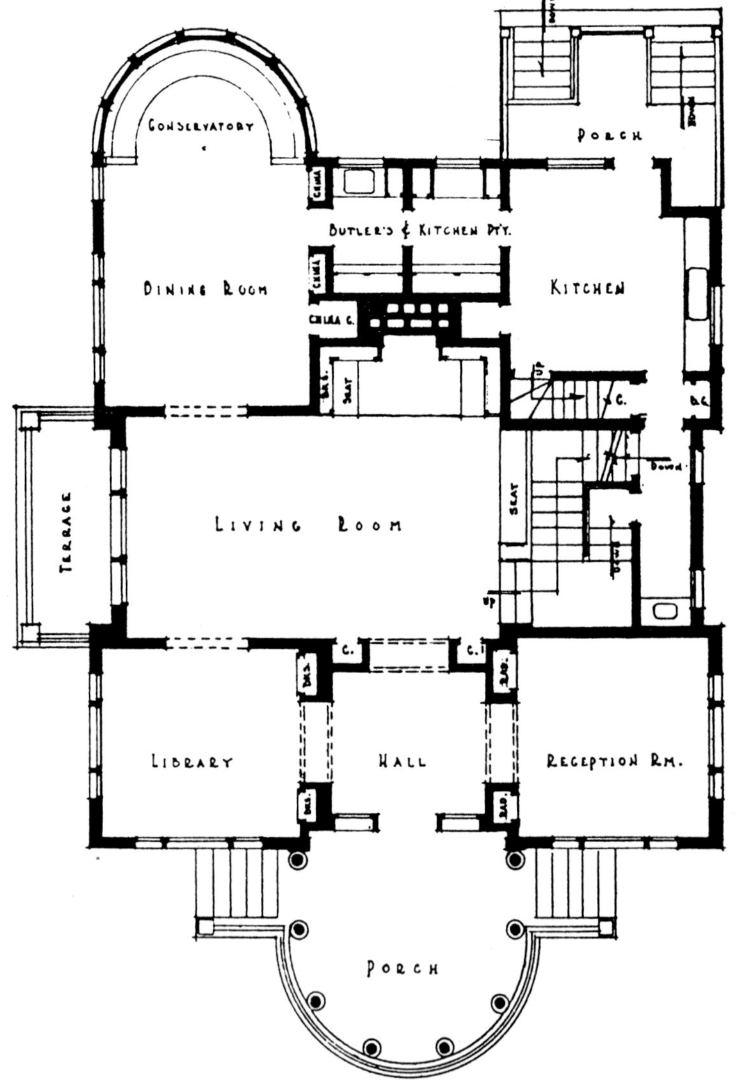

To prepare the building site, the cottage was carried across Third Street and set on a new basement of slender bricks [28]. The building process continued through 1903 and most of 1904 [29]. And the true extent of the project became known:

> The careful and exacting work on the brick setting is nearing completion. The magnitude and magnificence of the new residence begins to come out of the chaos and the indications are that the home will be a mansion unlike any other in the city for size, finish and cost.[25]

The man in charge of the exacting brickwork, Joseph M. Figueira, also could have been the general contractor, much in the manner of R. D. Lawrence.[26] S. J. Hanes, who served as Wright's representative, was a builder and architect whose office in the old Tinsley Building, at the southeast corner of the courthouse square, had once been Lincoln's office. He was known for having dared to expand the courthouse by raising the entire pile and inserting a new story. The procedure greatly amused R. D. Lawrence; in August 1899 he wrote his daughter in Oregon that the courthouse had reached 11 feet in the air without cracking. "I had hoped it would fall down," he wrote, "but it won't." What may have recommended Hanes to

---

[24]Clearly, the Dana house plan cannot be described accurately by the academic concepts of "cruciform" or "pinwheel" shapes. It bears likenesses also to the plan of Wright's house of 1899–1900 for Helen Husser in Chicago—which may explain why Wright liked to backdate the Dana house to 1899.

[25]*The Springfield News*, March 14, 1903, p. 5.

[26]Figueira (1873–1953) was first a bricklayer, then a masonry contractor, then general superintendent of the Springfield park system and, beginning in 1927, commissioner of public health and safety. "His skilled hands laid the bricks on the old Susan Lawrence Dana mansion," the *Illinois State Journal* commented in an editorial of June 6, 1953, two days after his death.

27. *Dining room, preliminary presentation drawing.*

28. *Foundation work, looking west; cottage and carriage house in background.*

29. *New walls around the old villa, looking northwest.*

30. *Early view, looking northwest.*

31. *Early view, looking southwest.*

Wright, however, was the curious coincidence that Mrs. Hanes, the former Ida May Murray, was a daughter of the judge who so accommodated Mrs. Dana in the matter of her father's estate.[27]

Her haste to spend his fortune nevertheless claimed its toll. Despite her immediate enthusiasm for the new house, she suffered doubts. In the summer of 1904 she resorted to spiritualists and mediums to solicit reassurance from the beyond, and her spirit-letters proved revelatory in a way she could hardly have intended:

> Papa, do you know all about the new house and are you pleased with it? Did I handle your will the way you wanted me to? I did the best I could.
>
> *Susie, I love the new house—Ed and I often visit there together. You handled the will all right, Susie, and I was able to help you—have no fear for the future, dear—*

So far as visitors from among the living, they began to arrive in October. The social season started with the Christmas holidays, when the studio window at the south terrace could perform its special function of admitting a very large Christmas tree. Those persons who chose to attend a charity bazaar on December 20 and 21 also arrived by the south terrace, a convenient way of screening them from the main house. They paid 25 cents for admittance.[28]

Other housewarmings—for the Woman's Club,

[27]Hanes (1862–1946), in the years 1902–04, identified himself in city directories as an "architect and superintendent." His third-floor corner office in the Tinsley Building of 1840–41 at the southwest corner of Sixth and Adams Streets had been Lincoln's office from 1843 to 1847. He married Judge Murray's daughter in 1884; their son Murray Hanes (1887–1984) writes in a typescript memoir of 1971–72 (now in the Lincoln Library, Springfield) that S. J. Hanes "became an associate of Mr. Wright on the so-known Lawrence-Dana home on South Fourth Street . . .. I recall that Mr. Wright was about to start the Larkin Soap Building, in Buffalo, and that he pleaded with my father to come with him on this project."

[28]The spirit-letters survive in the Bice Collection. *The Springfield News* reported on Oct. 3, 1904, p. 3, that Mrs. Dana had been entertaining guests from New York, Vienna and elsewhere. For the charity bazaar, see ibid., Dec. 20, 1904, p. 3.

32. *Dana house, looking southwest.*

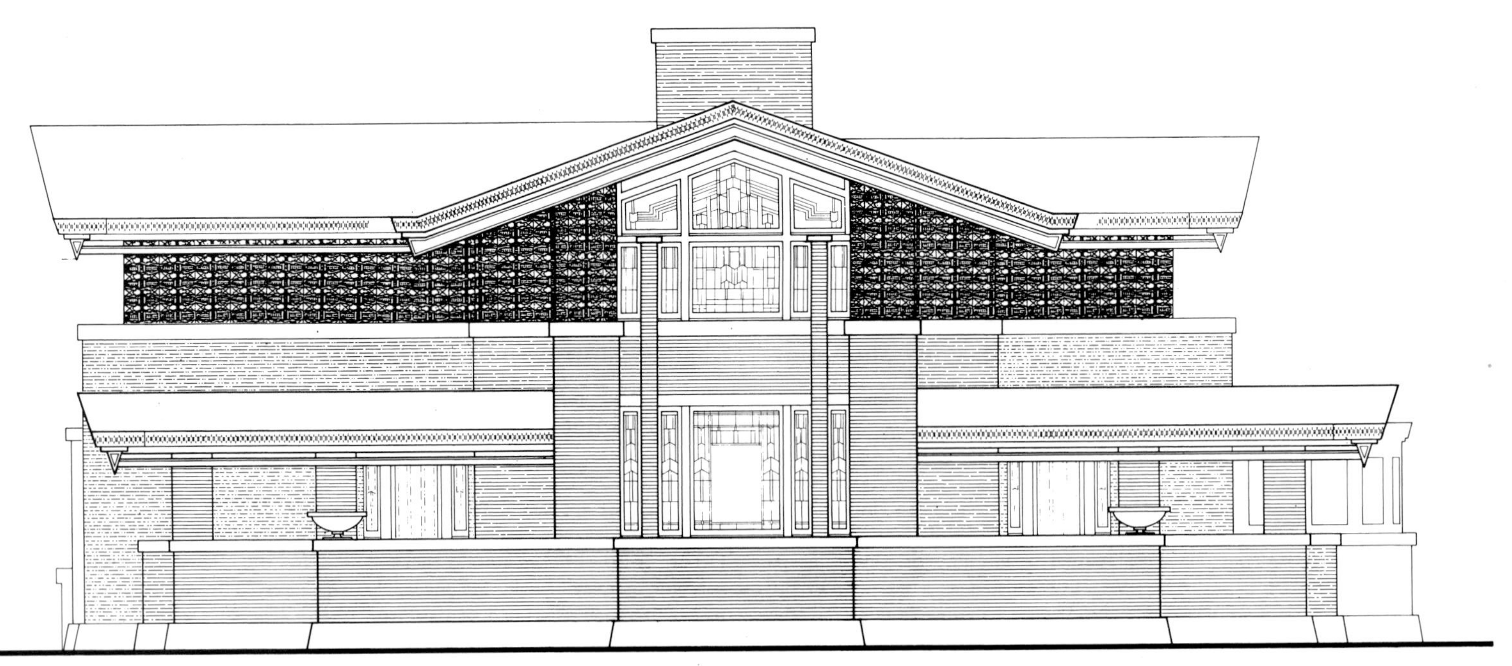

33. *East front, elevation.*

34. *East front.*

35. *Presentation drawing.*

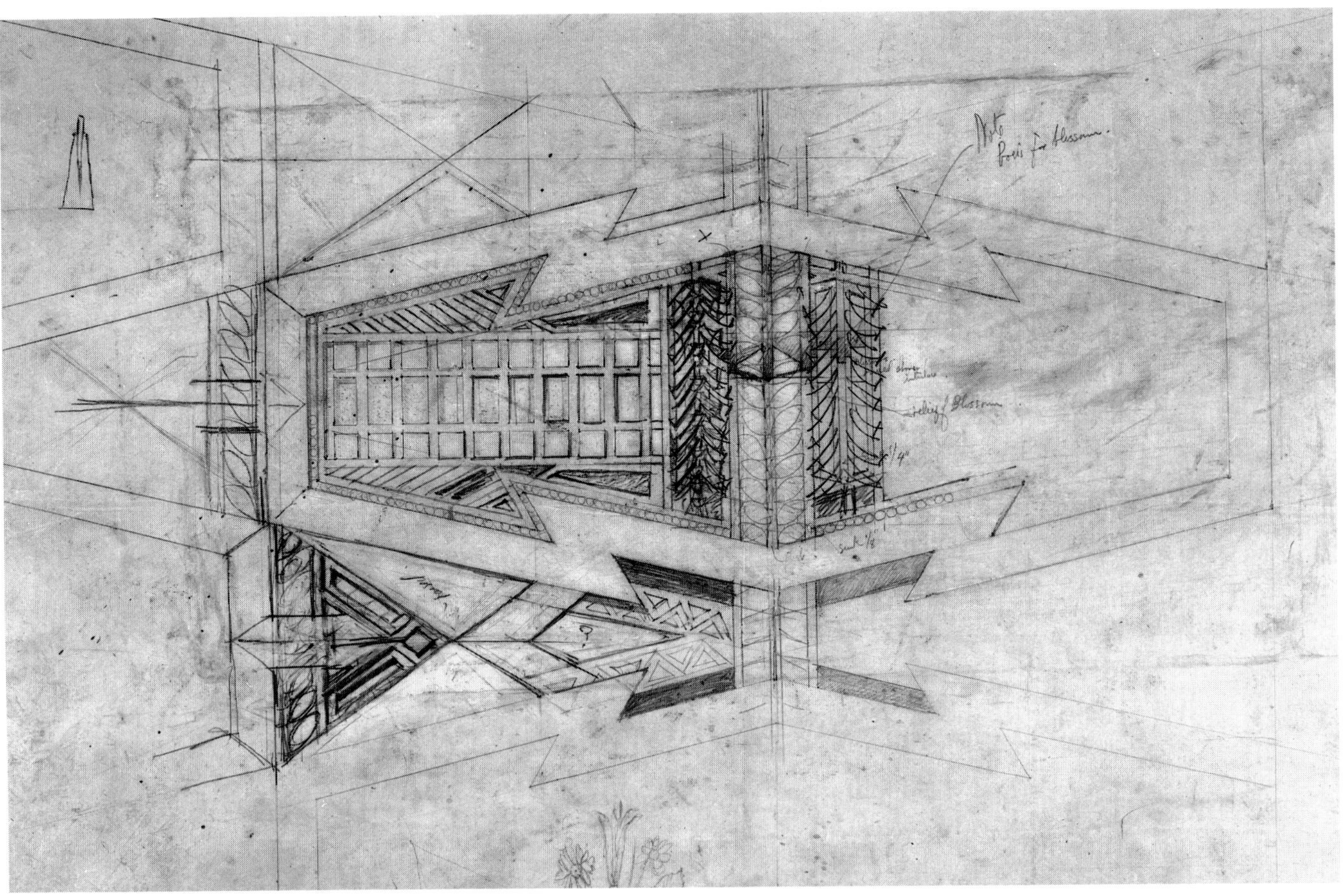

36. *Sketch for frieze pattern.*

of accent blocks (as Wright called them) and the other of flashing diagonals that follow the pitch of the roof. Hence the frieze mimics what it appears not to support. On a different drawing, Wright noted later that he had been thinking of a "cast metal frieze" or even a "bronze frieze." But he settled for reinforced plaster [37]. Colored bronze and green by a series of tints with metallic flake, the frieze imitates the verdigris of the copper cornice and gutter. The frieze and cornice together thus mediate between the red tiles of the roof and the grayish cream-colored bricks of the walls below.[4] The cornice in turn responds to the frieze by echoing its pattern of accent blocks [38]. At the salient corners, where the cornice flares outward and seems to kick upward, it in fact remains horizontal. Wright has fooled the eye.

The long south front unfurls like a Chinese handscroll from right to left [39, 40]. In scheme, it resembles Wright's project of 1900 for "A Home in a Prairie Town": a veranda, the central block with a two-story space, the entrance arch, a long hall or corridor, the courtyard and carriage house. Inspired by the horizontal, or what the critic Montgomery Schuyler was pleased to see as the "Rhapsodie Prairiale" in Wright's early work, the Dana house rests on the land as if some large recumbent figure.[5] In 1903, soon after he joined the Oak Park studio, Charles E. White, Jr., wrote his friend in Vermont:

> W. says all of his design was suggested by the prairies on which they [sic] are built—he is "thoroughly saturated with the spirit of the prairie"—and doesn't think he could easily design work for a hilly country.[6]

[4]"The green color of the copper in connection with stone or tiles or even wood is always beautiful," Wright wrote in 1928; see *Frank Lloyd Wright on Architecture* (New York, 1941), p. 106. In earlier years he had designed patterned friezes for the W. H. Winslow, Isidore Heller and Helen Husser houses. A note on a working drawing for the Dana house specifies "75 squares of tile," or enough to roof 7500 square feet. It was supplied by the Ludowici Roofing Tile Co. of Chicago.

[5]"An Architectural Pioneer: Review of the Portfolios Containing the Works of Frank Lloyd Wright" [1912], in *American Architecture and Other Writings*, ed. W. H. Jordy and Ralph T. Coe (New York, 1964), p. 315. Wright notably said his "Usonian" houses of the 1930s and later were "shaped like polliwogs"; see The Natural House (New York, 1954), p. 165. Of the Guggenheim Museum of 1943–59 he wrote, "It can do nearly everything but move and seems to do even that when you look at it"; see *Frank Lloyd Wright: The Guggenheim Correspondence* (Carbondale, Ill., 1986), p. 63.

[6]"Letters, 1903–1906, by Charles E. White, Jr. from the Studio of Frank Lloyd Wright," ed. Nancy K. Morris Smith, *Journal of Architectural Education XXV* (Fall 1971), p. 104. Wright often proved far from adept at acknowledging hilly sites in his building plans.

37. *Frieze detail.*

38. *Cornice and gutter detail.*

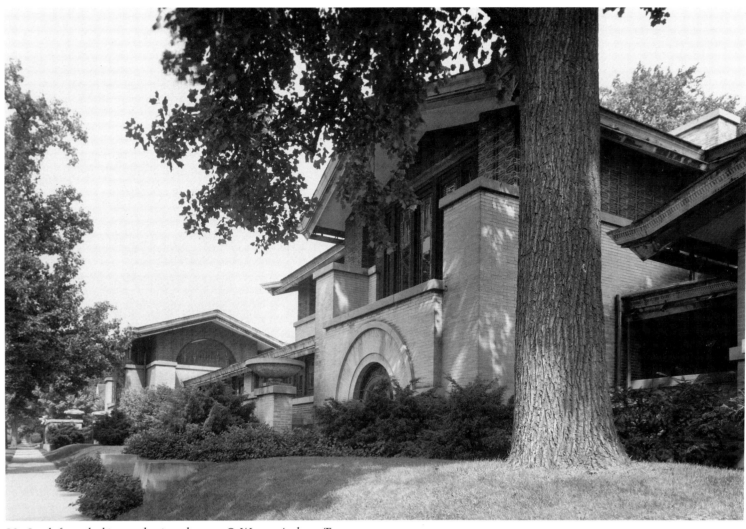

39. *South front, looking predominantly west.* © *Wayne Andrews/Esto.*

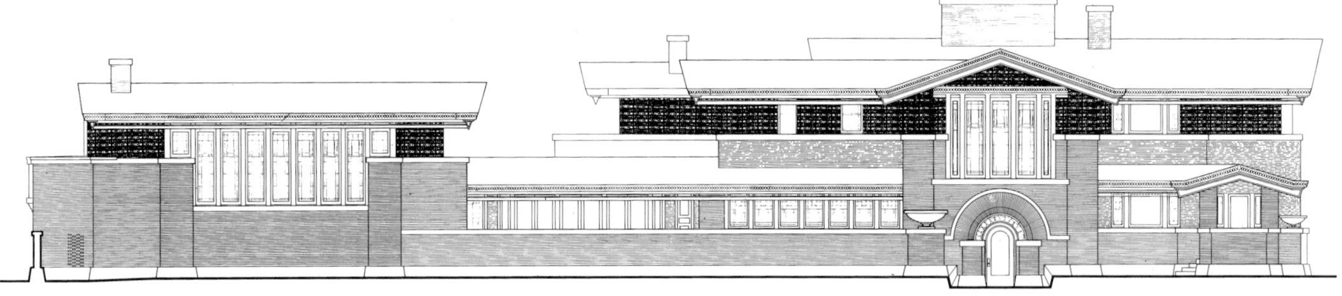

40. *South elevation.*

Mere nostalgia cannot account for the paradox of a city house that consumes its site to honor a vanished landscape: Wright believed that life within a broadened building would likewise be "broadened, made more free because of sympathetic freedom of plan and structure."[7]

Yet the lengthened outlines embrace certain basic conflicts. The entrance arch contests with the gable

[7]Wright, "Organic Architecture Looks at Modern Architecture," the *Architectural Record CXI* (May 1952), p. 150. His feeling for landscape and freedom can be compared with the famous dictum of Frederick Law Olmsted and Calvert Vaux in their 1866 report on Prospect Park in Brooklyn: " . . . *a sense of enlarged freedom* is to all, at all times, the most certain and the most valuable gratification afforded by a park"; see *Landscape into Cityscape*, ed. Albert Fein (Ithaca, N.Y., 1968), p. 98.

above and the post-and-lintel structure in between, and a similar juxtaposition occurs at the east wall of the studio, where a gable surmounts the arch of the lunette and the arch encloses a post-and-lintel frame for suspended panels of glass [41]. All of Ruskin's "three good architectures" come together as though Mrs. Dana's building program specified an embarrassment of riches.[8] And still the house is infused with the righteous spirit of reform; the long clean straight line, Wright said, signified "rectitude."[9] The concrete caps and beltcourses are so finely cast as to be commonly mistaken for cut stone, and the raked mortar beds and narrow bricks (nearly 12 inches long but little more than 2 inches high) everywhere accentuate the linear.

The studio—lightly tethered to the main house by the corridor, porch and south terrace—asserts a rigor of its own [42]. As another manifesto of the new

[8]John Ruskin, The Stones of Venice, vol. 2 (London, 1853), p. 213. Wright tacitly confessed the problem when he presented the Dana house in his 1911 Berlin publication as if the east front of the studio repeated the design of the east front of the main house. H. P. Berlage noted the conflict between the horizontality of the Dana house and its arches and vaulted rooms; see his essay in *The Life-Work of the American Architect Frank Lloyd Wright* (Dover reprint as *Frank Lloyd Wright: The Complete 1925 "Wendingen" Series*, New York, 1992), p. 83.

[9]*Frank Lloyd Wright: Collected Writings*, vol. 2, p. 213.

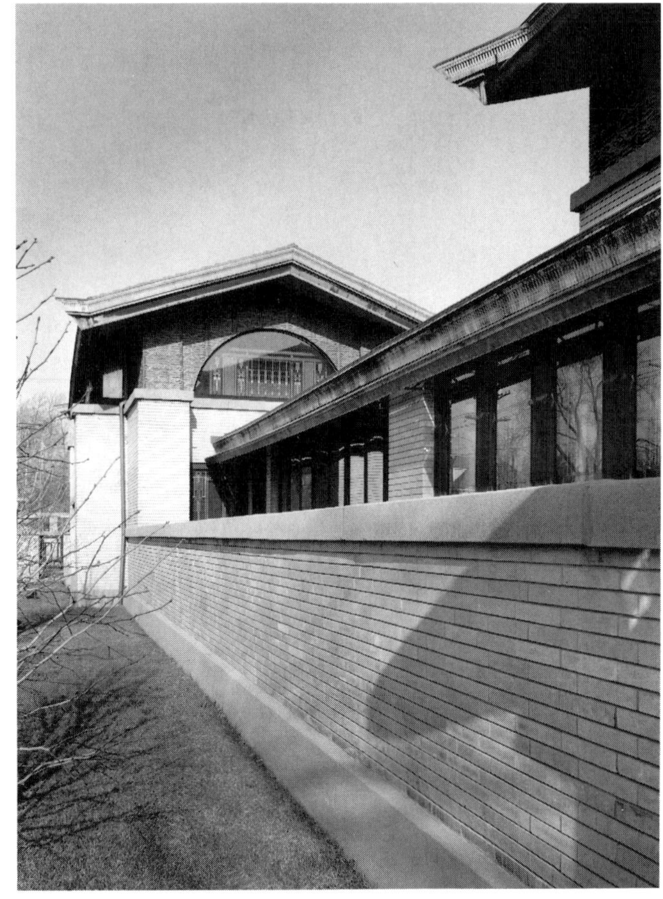

41. *East face of studio.*

42. *Studio, looking northeast, about 1950.*

43. *West face of studio.*

principles, it looks truly built to "liberate and expand, not contain and confine."[10] The pierlike shapes fall short of the eaves, the frieze and tall casements hardly seem capable of any burden, and the roof thus declares its independence of the walls. In the oddly masklike west face, the masonry wall clearly outweighs the windows of the corbeled bay [43]. But with the upper corners so radically opened and shaded, the rift below the cornice grows even more dramatic. From perspectives farther within the garden court, the studio seems charged with energy and poised to advance in any of several directions [44]. Here, already, that Gothic spirit Wright would recommend in his Berlin publication of 1911 is beautifully revealed [45]. The purpose was not to recall a style of the past, he wrote, but to revive the organic spirit:

> I have observed that Nature usually perfects her forms; the individuality of the attribute is seldom sacrificed; that is, deformed or mutilated by co-operative parts. She rarely says a thing and tries to take it back at the same time.[11]

[10] Wright, *A Testament* (New York, 1957), p. 135.
[11] Wright, "In the Cause of Architecture," p. 160.

44. *Studio, looking southeast.*

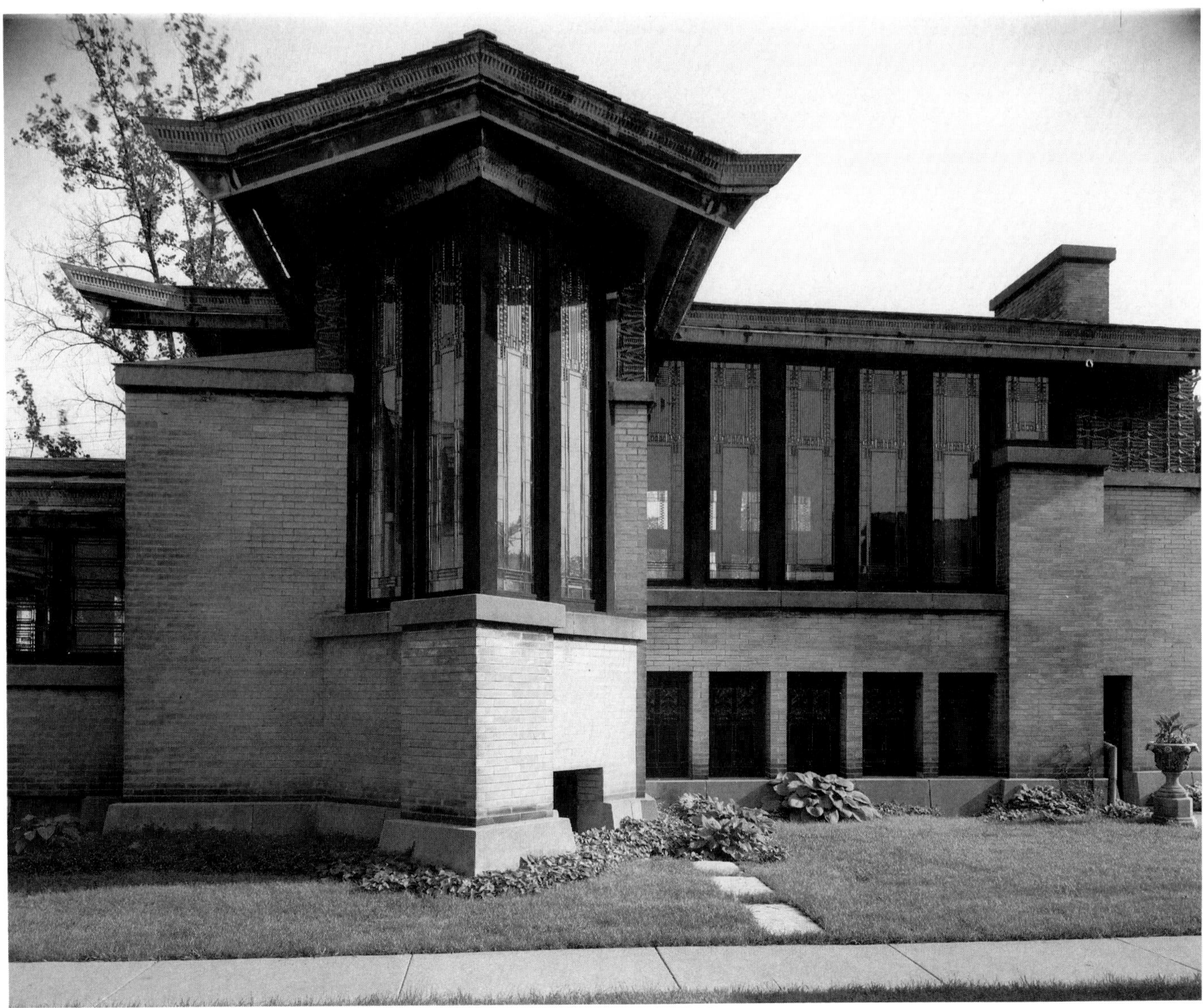

45. *Studio, looking south, 1955.*

To the east, the bedroom gables stand as broad towers above the doors to the court, and a long pool runs alongside the continuous casement windows of the conservatory [46]. A single limestone urn acknowledges the asymmetrical balance between the main part of the house and the kitchen wing, which so ponderously intrudes on the court [47]. The blind west wall of this veritable blockhouse rises to form the parapet of the servants' balcony [48]. At the north side, the house shows yet another face, one dominated by the projection of the pierlike shapes and breakfast bay more than 15 feet beyond the kitchen wall [49, 50]. Again the stepped massing and shadowed frieze set free the cantilevered roof.

A drawing for changes to the old carriage house and stable shows how Wright contrived to lower the roof lines, alter the windows and add the patterned copper cornice to bring the structure into harmony with the new house [51]. But he also screened most of the building with tall brick curtain walls surmounted by latticework of rough-sawn stiles and rails [52]. The new walls form a horse walk along the south side and a semicircular exercise enclosure at the east. More important, they give the old building a new and vital momentum.[12]

[12]Wright in several ways expressed his displeasure at the survival of the carriage house. In the plans he published in Berlin in 1910 and 1911, he placed the lower-floor plan of the studio wing where the carriage house should have been indicated; and in examining a photograph of the garden court by Maynard Parker (cf. Fig. 127) he scratched-over even the new brick curtain-wall with pen and ink. His idea of simplicity entailed the complete coordination of perfected parts into an organic whole. "Plainness was not necessarily simplicity," he wrote in *An Autobiography* (New York, 1943), p. 144.

Early views of the garden court show a profusion of hollyhocks that ornament and soften the planes of the 8-foot walls; see Leigh Gross Day, *In Shadow-Town* (Akron, Ohio, 1907) and *Borderland And The Blue Beyond* (Akron, Ohio, 1908).

46. *Garden court, looking east.*

47. *Kitchen wing, looking southeast.*

52. *Carriage house and stable, looking northwest.*

In Another World

HOW WOULD ARCHITECTURE converse with nature in a place where so little of nature survived? A city house, Wright said, presented a special challenge:

> A building should appear to grow easily from its site and be shaped to harmonize with its surroundings if Nature is manifest there, and if not try to make it as quiet, substantial and organic as She would have been were the opportunity Hers.[1]

Hence the central paradox: Wright liberated the Dana house to a landscape no longer there, then reconstituted nature metaphorically by conceiving the interior as an abstract equivalent of the lost prairie. How poignant it was that just as he built her an idealized environment Mrs. Dana turned to a place presumed to lie beyond the visible. The second and last person to own the house, Charles C. Thomas, evidently understood it better. He said it was like being in another world [53–55].

To be sure, the house gives fair notice. The entrance engages the spirit, introduces themes, hints at further surprises and shapes a passage from the everyday world into the realm of art [56, 57]. The walkway cuts through the terrace to define a space for pause or assembly at the front door. An elevated and oversized urn nicely inverts the curve of the entrance arch. Bronze gates once guarded the door with grilles of closely ranked stiles and accent blocks, screens like that of the player organ in the living-hall gallery [58].[2]

The brick masonry, keen and skilled, honors the memory of R. D. Lawrence [59]. Chubby piers compress the entrance in calculated contrast to the expansive spaces to come. They also retreat from their ostensible load, the compound arch that so buoyantly leaps beyond them. A butterfly wreath or transom—as Wright described it—forms the fan at the front door and again at the vestibule door [60, 61]. It is only the first of a long series of inventions in art glass more elegant than those from any other moment in Wright's career.[3] The panes of green and gold and brown speak of autumn days when the prairie is ripe and butterflies flourish. The pattern transforms the insect into a geometric construction, then multiplies it into a crystalline chain 11 inches wide. Significantly, it is the structural system that asserts control:

> The windows usually are provided with characteristic straight line patterns absolutely in the flat and usually severe. The nature of the glass is taken into

[1]Wright, "In the Cause of Architecture," p. 157.

[2]The gates are in storage because they had been removed by 1910, the approximate date to which the house has been restored.

[3]The commonplace judgment that the windows Wright designed for the Coonley Playhouse represent his most important work in glass should not be accepted. The glass of the Dana house is more imaginative, more complex, more subtly colored and more varied. It comprises hundreds of windows, transoms, doors, ceiling panels, wall-mounted lamps, suspended lamps, standing lamps and, finally, a unique hanging glass screen.

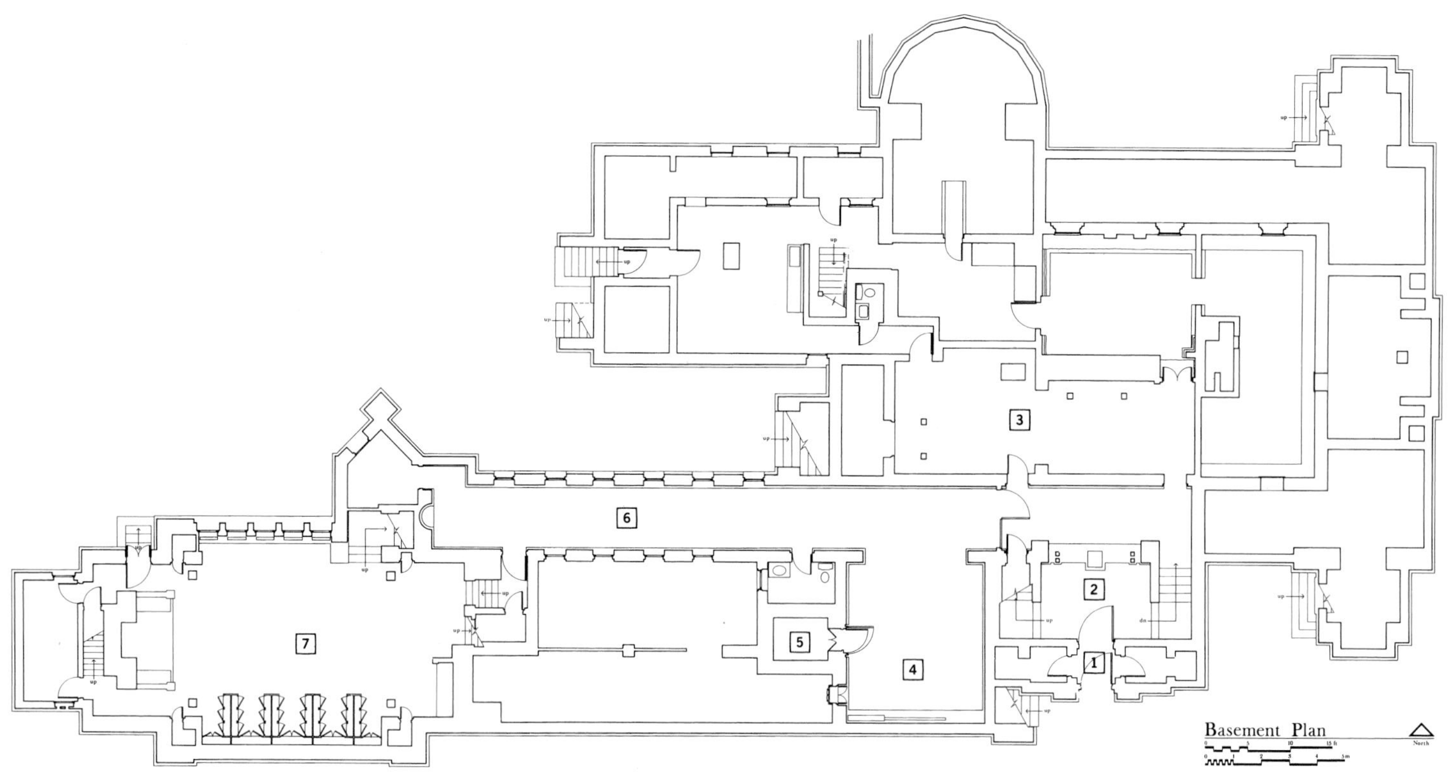

53. *Basement plan: (1) vestibule; (2) entry; (3) cloakrooms; (4) billiard room; (5) safety vault; (6) bowling alley; (7) library.*

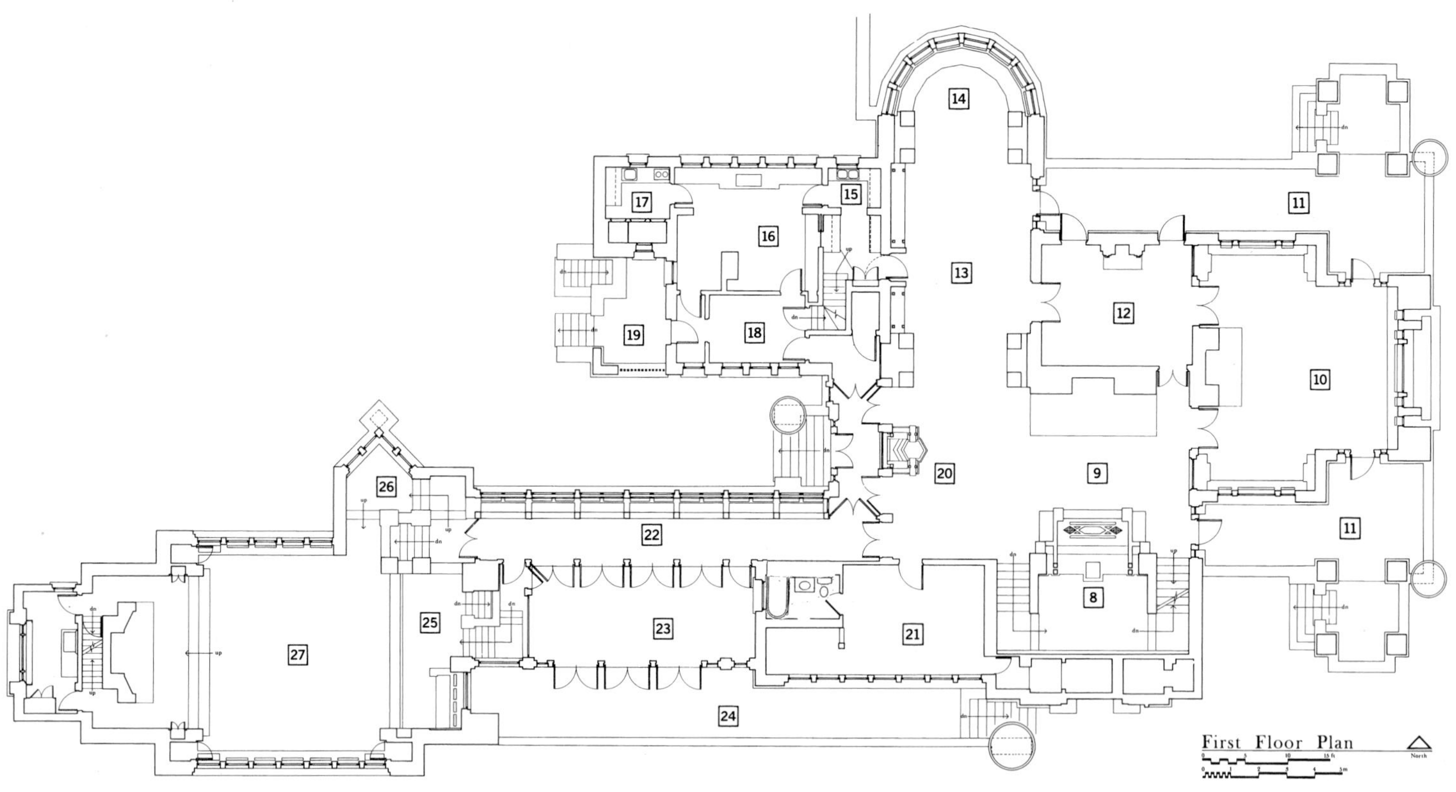

54. *First-floor plan: (8) "Flower in the Crannied Wall"; (9) living hall; (10) living room; (11) verandas; (12) sitting room, or den; (13) dining room; (14) breakfast alcove; (15) serving pantry; (16) kitchen; (17) pantry and refrigerator room; (18) servants' dining room; (19) service porch; (20) "Moon Children" fountain; (21) bedroom suite; (22) corridor and conservatory; (23) porch; (24) south terrace; (25) stairwell to library; (26) stair landing to studio; (27) studio.*

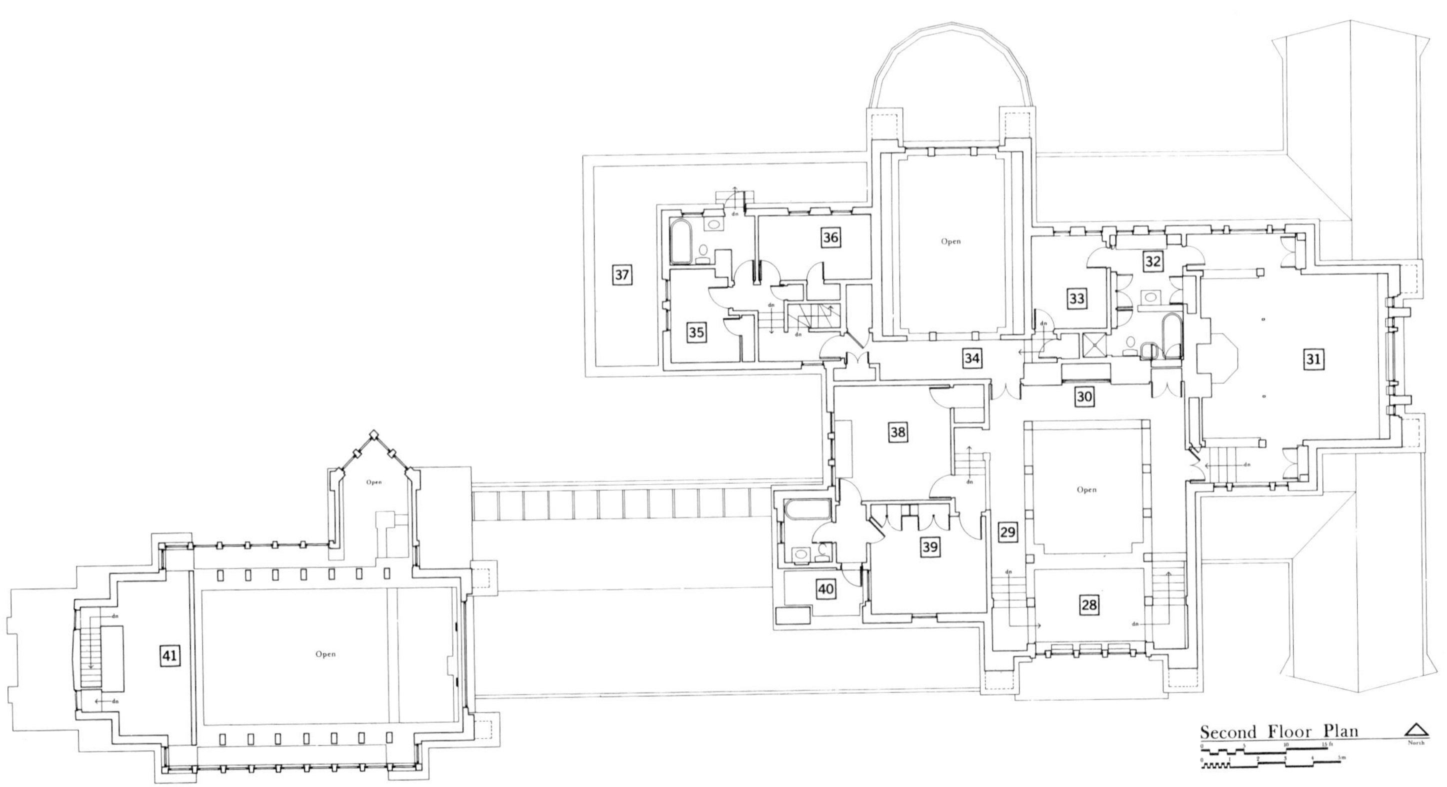

55. *Second-floor plan: (28) landing above living hall; (29) gallery; (30) player organ; (31) master bedroom; (32) dressing alcove; (33) nursery; (34) hall; (35) west servant's room; (36) north servant's room; (37) servants' porch; (38) bedroom; (39) dressing room; (40) loggia; (41) balcony.*

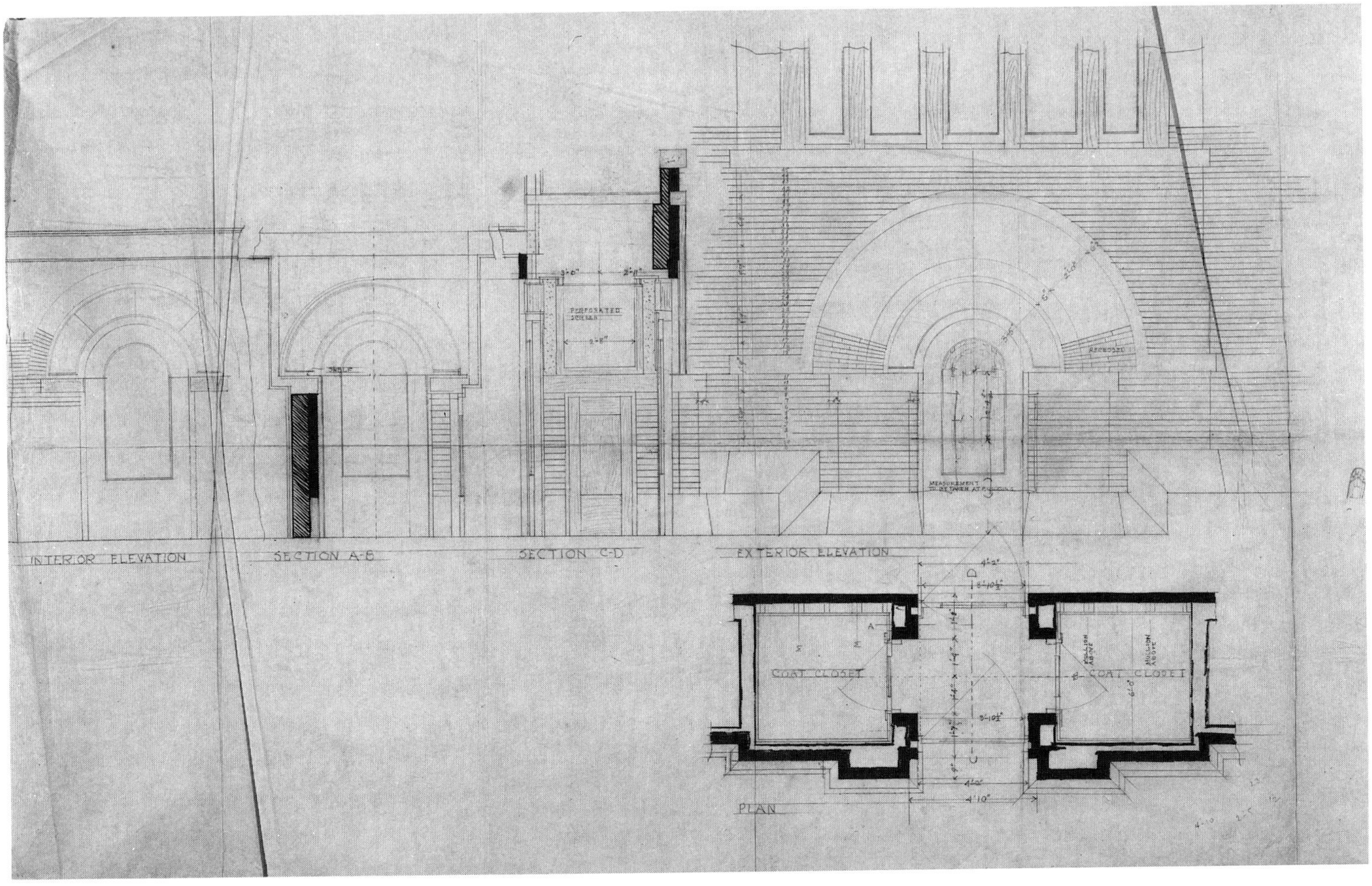

56. *Entrance and vestibule, plan, elevations and sections.*

57. *Entrance, looking north.*

58. *Design for gates.*

59. *Brickwork at entrance.*

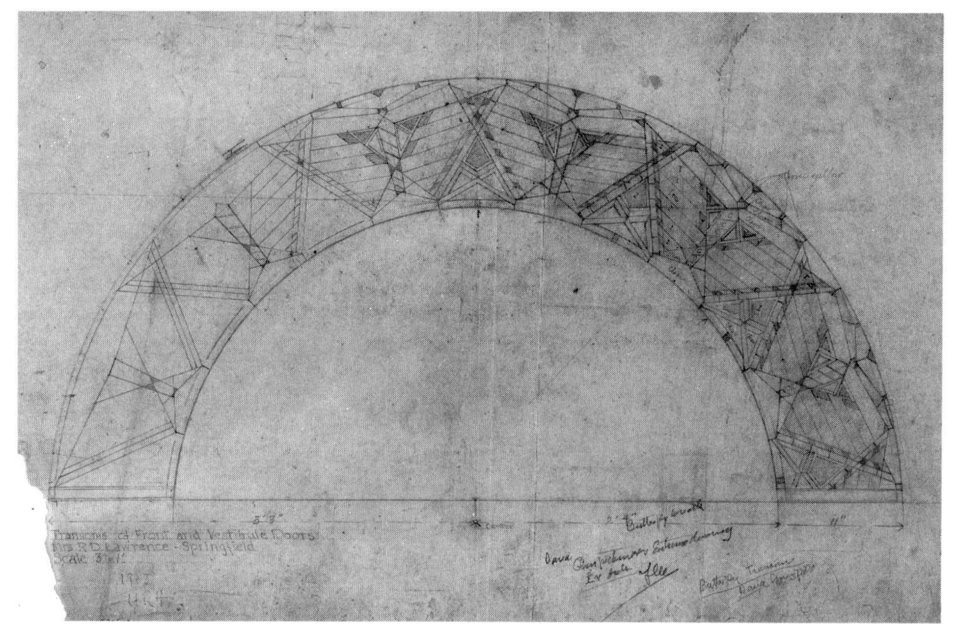

60. *Transom design.*

61. *Butterfly transoms.*

62. *Vestibule.*

63. *Vault of vestibule.*

> account in these designs as is also the metal bar used in their construction, and most of them are treated as metal "grilles" with glass inserted forming a simple rhythmic arrangement of straight lines and squares made as cunning as possible so long as the result is quiet.[4]

Wright's glass patterns become more intricate if the outdoor vistas lack charm; again, architecture takes the place of lost nature. Some say the butterfly motif derives from the old fireplace front in the Victorian sitting room, where nine small butterflies are carved into the stone. But the sense of wings resides more basically in the cantilevered roof of the new house; paradoxically, Wright accentuated the horizontal as "the true earth-line of human life, indicative of freedom" and yet celebrated flight as the supreme expression of freedom in space.[5]

The diminutive vestibule (its doors $4^1/_2$ feet apart and the closets only 5 feet high) already is graced by that attention to detail so characteristic of the house, and its space is greatly enriched by a vaulted ceiling of art glass [62, 63]. The entry is nearly four times

[4]Wright, "In the Cause of Architecture," p. 161. He wrote "Brass Screen—Brass Grille, glass filled" on a drawing for the ensemble of glass doors and windows behind the living-hall fountain of the Dana house.

[5]Wright, *An Autobiography* (1943), p. 349. Coincidentally, in 1903 the two Wright brothers achieved the first successfully sustained flight of a heavier-than-air and engine-powered craft. Winged figures of an academic sort had appeared in Adler & Sullivan's projects of 1892 for the Trust & Savings Building in St. Louis and the Victoria Hotel in Chicago, as well as in their Transportation Building for the World's Columbian Exposition of 1893, in Chicago; and again in Sullivan's Bayard Building of 1897–98 in New York. Wright's more structural sense of wings becomes particularly apparent in his conception of the column-section for the Johnson Wax Building of 1936–39, in Racine, Wis.; in the floor-section for the Johnson Research Tower of 1946–50; in the "Butterfly-Wing Bridge" project of 1949–53 for San Francisco Bay; and finally in the sketch he made in 1958 for a personal "Heliocopter" that would move like a winged seed of a dandelion.

64. *Entry, looking northeast.*

65. *Wall-mounted lamp.*

larger. It shapes another place of pause and expectation [64]. The penumbral light is typical; Wright wrote that he grouped the casement windows of his prairie houses into rhythmic sequence to secure "all the light and air and prospect the most rabid client could wish," but the Dana house looks inward and its light remains as hushed as that of dusk.[6] The wall-mounted lamps of only eight candlepower glow like evening fireflies [65]. To some extent they follow a drawing made by Walter Burley Griffin in the spring of 1904, but Wright has refined the design to make it at once more simple and more elegant.[7]

Straight lines rule the entire entry: the casework, armchairs, even the masonry walls of bricks still more slender than those of the exterior. Narrow stripes in stained oak cross the walls to hurry along the horizontal. To the plainest of moldings Wright gave purpose, because he saw in every detail the spirit of the whole:

> Simplicity in art, rightly understood, is a synthetic positive quality, in which we may see evidence of mind, breadth of scheme, wealth of detail, and withal a sense of completeness found in a tree or a flower.[8]

Evidence of mind and breadth of scheme give the details their thoroughly architectonic character. The armchairs are only 22 inches high, but they gain the same monumental strength as the Larkin Building; the casepieces, which combine umbrella stands with cabinets and shelves, can forecast the majestic order of Unity Temple. Hence the integrity of the house challenges every part to contribute heartily to the whole. Any detail wrenched from its place and regarded as an isolated object of the decorative arts, not to say commodity, cries out as an orphaned child.

The preliminary drawings had shown a niche probably designed for a sculpture, but when Wright turned the living hall to the south he envisioned a small Winged Victory positioned instead at the entry, although faced toward the living-hall fireplace [66]. In a second perspective study, a sculpture indistinctly drawn appears to be addressed the opposite way, as though to preside over the entry as a heraldic figure [67]. This was to become the "Flower in the Crannied Wall," an allegory of the manifold and ultimately mysterious relations between architecture and nature [68]. Typically enough, John Lloyd Wright found amusement in recalling the nude model he had glimpsed at the age of 11:

> Papa kept a naked woman on his drafting-room balcony. I saw her through the high windows opening over the flat gravel roof. She was pretty and had freckles. I tore across the street to get my playmate, Cliff McHugh. Dickie Bock, the sculptor, squinted his eyes in her direction, then pressed the clay into curves like those she was made of. Papa came to the balcony and scrutinized Dickie's work. All of a sudden he ripped it apart. Dickie watched him with big tears streaming down his cheeks, then proceeded to do the parts over to suit Dad.
>
> Papa spied us, chased us off the roof, brought us in and sat us down next to Dickie. Here we could get the artistic viewpoint. Papa said Dickie was modeling a statue for the Dana house to symbolize Tennyson's immortal lines:

[6]Wright, "In the Cause of Architecture," p. 160.

[7]For a rough sketch of the Griffin proposal, see "Letters, 1903–1906, by Charles E. White, Jr.," p. 106. The wall-mounted lamps, in brass, are about 13 inches tall and $3^1/_2$ inches wide. Wright used the same lamps in the Francis W. Little house in Peoria, Ill., and the George Barton and W. R. Heath houses in Buffalo, N.Y. Specifications for "Electric Work" at the Dana house called for 371 lights of all types and for an intercommunicating telephone system with nine stations.

[8]Wright, "The Art and Craft of the Machine," n. p. Wright also used wood stripes across bricks in the Helen Husser house of 1899–1900.

66. *Living hall with Winged Victory, presentation drawing.*

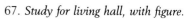

67. *Study for living hall, with figure.*

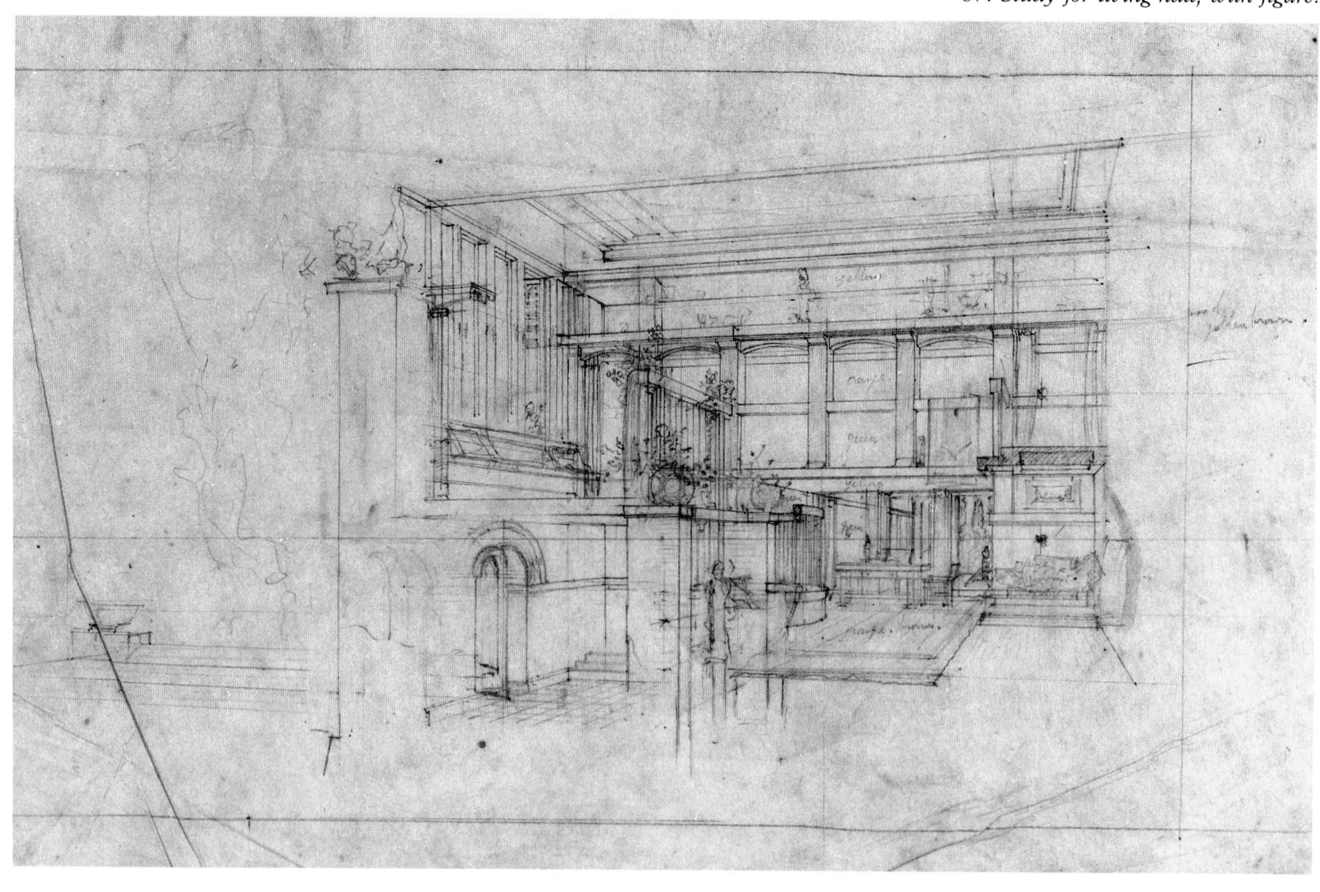

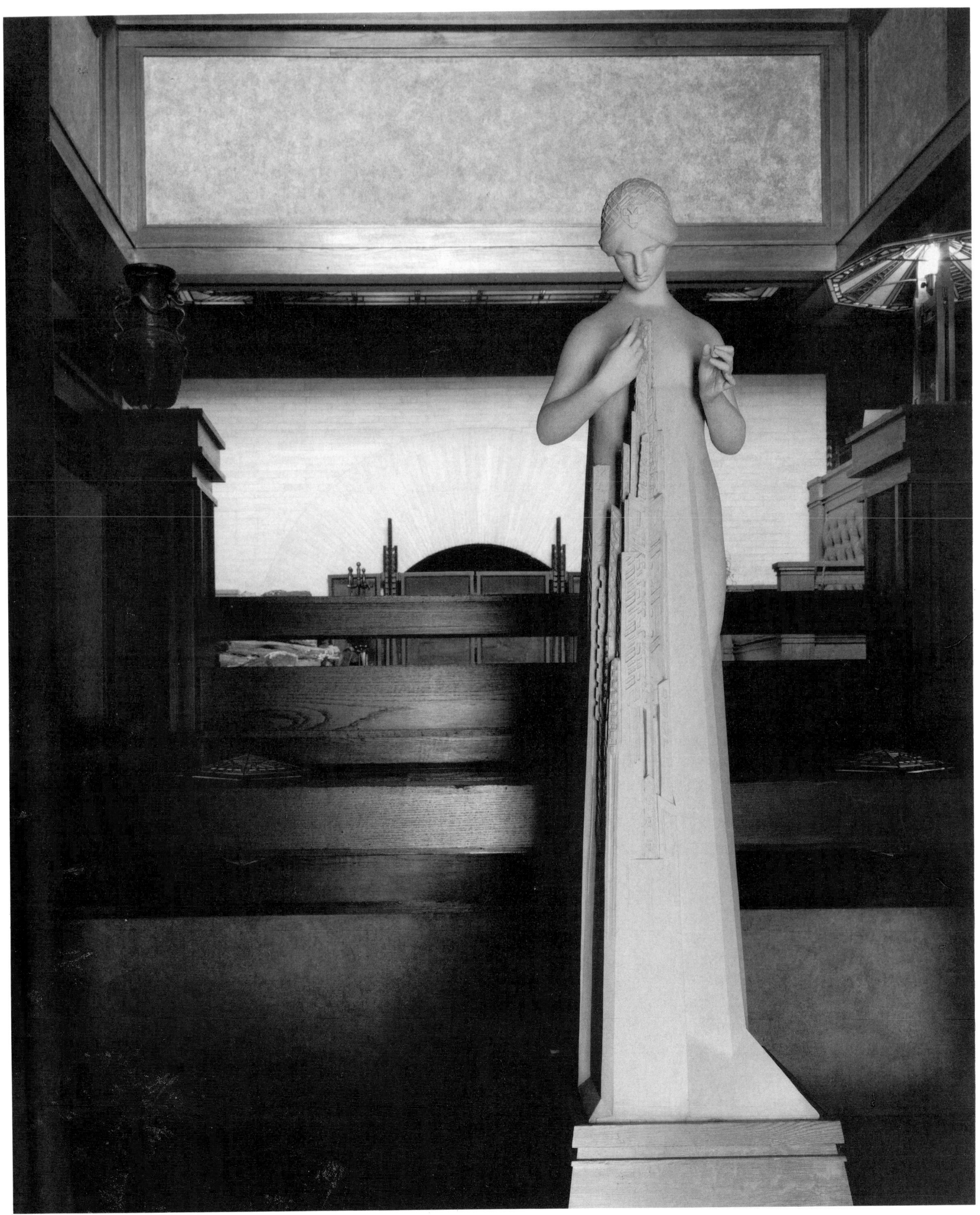

68. *"Flower in the Crannied Wall," looking north into living hall.*

69. *Statue of John Wright holding goldenrod.*

Flower in the crannied wall,
I pluck you out of the crannies,
I hold you here, root and all, in my hand,
Little flower—but if I could understand
What you are, root and all, and all in all,
I should know what God and man is.

We lost interest.[9]

The figure culminated a long effort by Wright to express the sources of his art. Bock undertook the assignment after an older and less tractable artist, Albert Louis Van den Berghen, failed to grasp what Wright so vaguely had in mind. Van den Berghen claimed to have worked for Louis Sullivan many years earlier, and he was spending a day or two a week at the Oak Park studio in May 1904, when Charles E. White, Jr., wrote of Bock's arrival:

> One late acquaintance, however, which gives me much pleasure, is Richard Bock, Sculptor, who has moved to Oak Park, and will occupy the balcony [of the studio]. He has decided to put himself under Mr. W's criticism for a period, as it is his ambition to become a strictly Architectural Sculptor. He will do work for the Buffalo building [the Larkin Building] . . ..[10]

Bock, too, had worked for Sullivan, but only once, in the winter of 1891–92, when he modeled ornaments and allegorical figures for the Schiller Theater in Chicago. That winter he first met Wright—whom he recalled as "a breezy young man, well groomed, with a definite self-assurance that was no doubt indicative of his destiny."[11] In 1897, Bock modeled the plaster frieze of Wright's house for Isidore Heller in Chicago, and also made a small portrait statue of Wright's son John holding goldenrod [69]. Bock proved malleable and eager to collaborate. The frieze panels of the Heller house in fact resembled a design of Wright's for the title page of a privately printed edition of *The Eve of St. Agnes*; Bock simply fused Wright's ornamental patterns with his own lithe female figures. Wright was pleased, and soon installed four extra panels at the drafting-room fireplace of his new Oak Park studio. Bock worked directly from Wright's drawing when he modeled the stork capitals for the studio entrance [70, 71].

Six years later, Bock faced a far more difficult task:

> As I had been busy and not available during this time, Frank was obliged to find someone else, and the sculptor who was working with him was a man named Vandenberg [sic], a talented but eccentric artist without any basic training. He wore his hair long and had a long beard cut in the image of Christ . . . .
>
> Frank called me in to straighten out the dilemma. He wanted me to do a standing figure for the entrance of the Dana house that Vandenberg [sic] had started but was unable to continue. Frank's idea for the figure was well conceived but far from solved. When I took it over there followed a long and tedious effort, in which as usual, we frictionized and fraternized, often coming to the verge of tears in our arguments for Frank could not make up his mind how it should be done. He was still under the thrall of Sullivan's style, which I worked very hard to break down. So we were building up and tearing down con-

[9]John Lloyd Wright, *My Father Who Is on Earth*, pp. 27–28.

[10]"Letters, 1903–1906, by Charles E. White, Jr.," p. 105. The elusive A. L. Van den Berghen, born in Belgium in 1850, came to America in 1876. Fragmentary records indicate that in 1889 his Ecce Homo, in papier-mâché, entered the Pennsylvania Academy of Fine Arts, in Philadelphia. In 1896 he exhibited three models for sculptures in the ninth annual exhibition of the Chicago Architectural Club. Also see the American Art Annual VI, ed. F. N. Levy (New York, 1908), p. 428.

[11]Richard W. Bock, *Memoirs of an American Artist*, ed. Dorathi Bock Pierre (Los Angeles, 1989), p. 46.

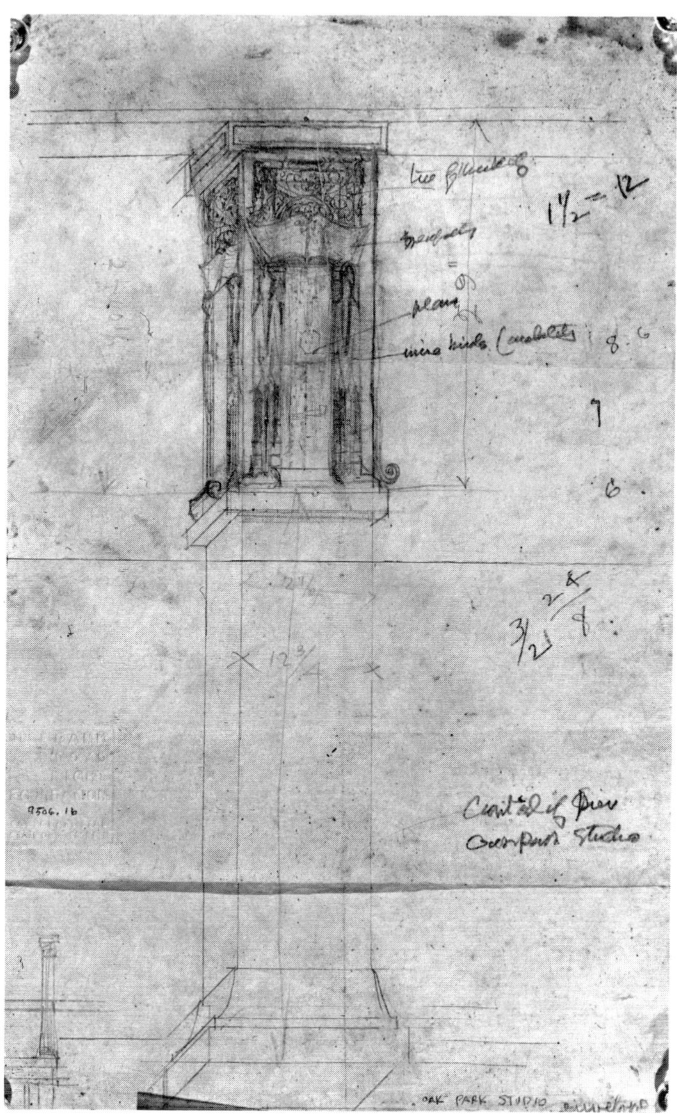

70. *Sketch for stork capitals.*

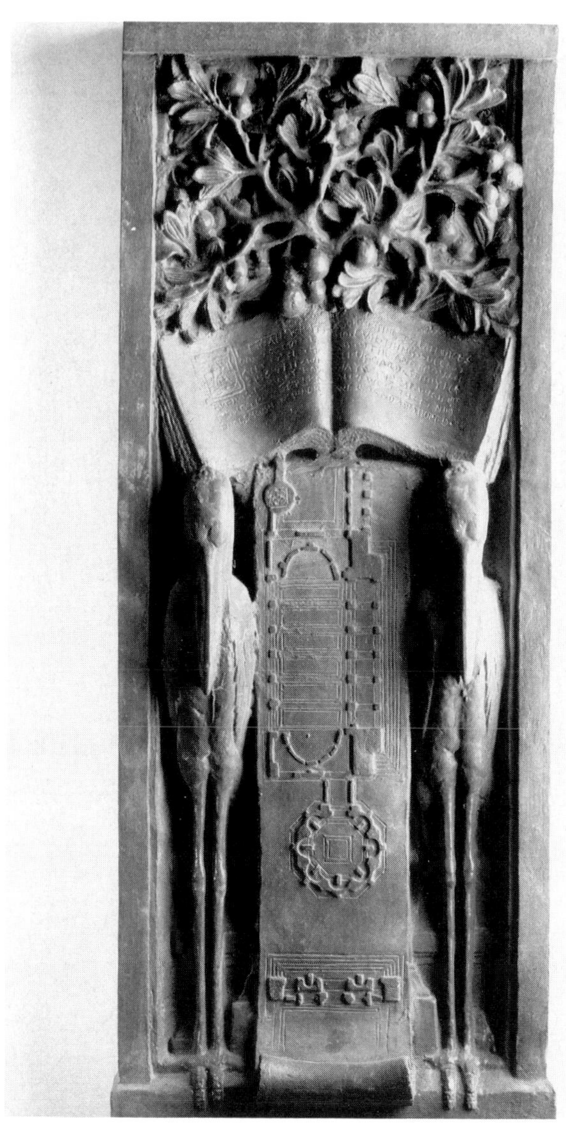

71. *Face of stork capital.*

> stantly. Finally he was called out of town on business for a number of days. During this time I was able to finish the entire figure. When he returned and saw what I had done, he beamed and threw his arms around me. "You have done it," he exclaimed, "you have done it, Dicky, you have done it. This is going to make you famous."[12]

Van den Berghen's mistake was to represent the poem much too literally. His figure, stiff as an archaic Greek stele, held a weirdly sinuous and overscaled plant. In contrast, Bock blended an idealized nude—his forte—with a compound pylon of geometric facets, a construction clearly in Wright's idiom. Bock's own preparatory sketch showed only the figure.[13]

Curiously, in the private edition of *The House Beautiful*, Wright already had quoted the verses from Tennyson alongside a page ornament, and had decorated the title page with a row of male figures bearing blocks of stone, an allegory of architecture [72]. The stork capitals at his studio represented another version of the same theme; the storks symbolized fertility, Wright said many years later, while the

[12]Ibid., p. 81. Also see Donald Parker Hallmark, "Chicago Sculptor Richard W. Bock: Social and Artistic Demands at the Turn of the Twentieth Century," PhD. diss., St. Louis University, 1980, pp. 202–208.

[13]The sketch is illustrated in Hallmark, "Chicago Sculptor Richard W. Bock," p. 209. The historian Mary Jane Hamilton has discovered a photograph of Van den Berghen at work on the balcony of the Oak Park studio modeling his version of the sculpture. "To me he always seemed to resemble a Gothic steeple," the sculptor Stanislav Szukalski recalled of Van den Berghen; see "Stanislav Szukalski's Lost Tune," *Chicago History XX* (1991), p. 57.

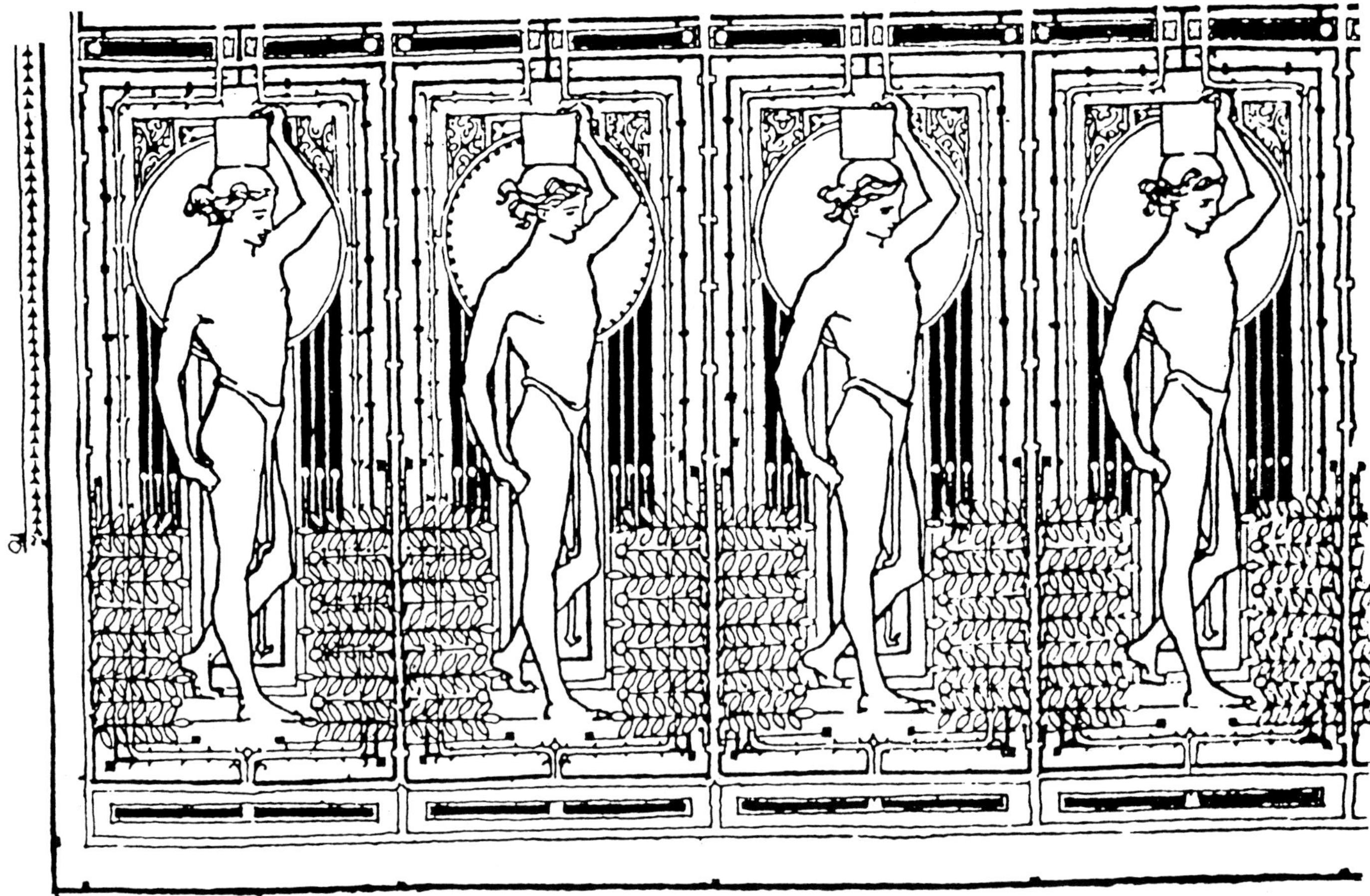

72. *Title-page figures.*

oak tree stood for life, and the plan and book of specifications of course signified architecture.[14] "Architecture" could not claim to be one of the nine muses of classical antiquity, but Giambologna's marble sculpture at the Bargello Palace in Florence had famously treated it so [73]. In 1891, after three years of study abroad, Bock rushed across Italy; he spent a day in Florence and visited the Bargello, but whether he pondered Giambologna's sculpture is a matter his memoirs leave unmentioned.[15] In any event, the symbolism of the piece is deplorably obvious. In one hand the muse holds a set-square, protractor and pair of dividers, and in the other a small drafting-board; her necklace may be a plumb line. By contrast, Bock's realization of the "Flower in the Crannied Wall" achieves a noble dignity, embodies many meanings and resists any simple or final interpretation. No wonder that Wright was so happy. The obvious was never enough. "The symbol is too literal," he wrote later. "It is become a form of Literature in the Arts."[16]

At first the muse at the Dana house entry seems engaged in constructing a fantastic spire that exults in the very process of its own creation. Yet the spire and the muse both emerge from the same compound of shafts. The muse may also represent the client, the patron of the arts who to that extent brought the

[14]Mark L. Peisch, *The Chicago School of Architecture*, p. 40. On his drawing for the stork capitals, Wright later wrote "wise birds"—probably a sarcasm that would support the notion that he was poking fun at the solemn, reactionary leaders of the Arts and Crafts movement, as reported by Robert C. Spencer, Jr., in "The Work of Frank Lloyd Wright," p. 65.

[15]The sculpture in the Bargello dates from ca. 1565–70. Giambologna, considered a master of contrapposto (the opposition of masses) or *figura serpintinata* (twisted like a serpent), was born in Flanders and named Jean Boulogne; see Charles Avery, *Giambologna: The Complete Sculpture* (Mt. Kisco, N.Y., 1987) and *Giambologna, 1529–1608: Sculptor to the Medici*, ed. Charles Avery and Anthony Radcliffe (London, 1978).

Giovanni Bandini (1540–1599) in 1568 carved a marble statue of "Architecture" for the tomb of Michelangelo at the church of Santa Croce in Florence. A bronze version of Giambologna's "Architecture," cast about 1580, is in the Museum of Fine Arts, Boston.

[16]*Frank Lloyd Wright: Collected Writings*, vol. 2, p. 212. "The literary mind has difficulty I find because Architecture is essentially pure abstraction," he wrote in 1944; see *Frank Lloyd Wright: The Guggenheim Correspondence*, p. 43. Much recent commentary on Wright's work has been almost entirely literary and irrelevant.

Bock's sculpture proved more significant and endearing than Wright's attempts ten years later, at the Midway Gardens in Chicago, to render the human figure itself as a geometric abstraction.

building into being. The immediate appeal of the figure speaks of the erotic basis of art, and the geometric spire of chevrons, triangles, rhomboids and squares can recall Stendhal's metaphor of falling in love, a leafless bough lifted from the salt pond astonishingly transformed by a glittering coat of crystals.[17] And then the verses from Tennyson, inscribed on the back of the sculpture together with several musical chords; their sense is much the same as that in a passage from Schopenhauer:

> . . . the inner being itself is present whole and undivided in everything in nature, in every living being. Therefore we lose nothing if we stop at any particular thing, and true wisdom is not to be acquired by our measuring the boundless world, or, what would be more appropriate, by our personally floating through endless space. On the contrary, it is acquired by thoroughly investigating any individual thing . . . .[18]

Strangely, the individual thing the muse investigates is not one of nature's innumerable models for art, but a geometric abstraction, an epitome of architecture. Conversely, the muse herself expresses the beauty of nature. Architecture and nature remain inseparable.[19]

Cast in terra-cotta at nearly life-size, the sculpture animates the vista into the lofty space of the living hall. An alternative vista, narrow and mysterious, penetrates to the basement corridor: a most radical way of expanding the space. Steps by the east wall lead down to the cloakrooms; those at the west wall rise to the living hall, 5½ feet above the entry [74]. The noble hall at first seems small, but the space primarily serves as a central place of dispersal—to the dining room, garden court, corridor and studio wing, bedroom suite, sitting room, living room, south veranda and finally the stairs to the second floor. Now the vistas are much deeper, more than 60 feet from the fountain at the west side of the living hall to the east wall of the living room, and nearly the same distance from the bedroom door to the north edge of the breakfast alcove. To the idea of an entrance hall transformed by an inglenook and stairwell into a living hall—a commonplace of the late nineteenth-century country house—Wright brought a new energy and dynamism.[20]

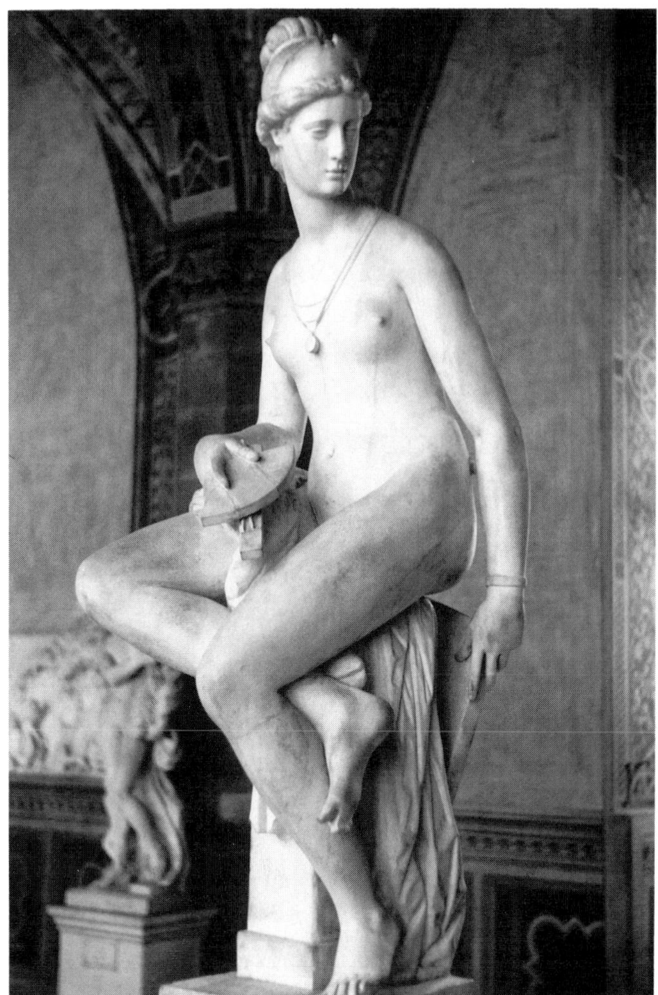

73. *"Architecture," by Giambologna, the Bargello, Florence.*

[17]Stendhal, *Love* [1822], tr. Gilbert and Suzanne Sale (Harmondsworth, England, 1975), p. 45. Wright described Sullivan's ornament as "that supreme, erotic, high adventure of the mind"; see "Louis H. Sullivan, His Work," *the Architectural Record* LVI (July 1924), p. 30. Also see *Genius and the Mobocracy*, p. 80. Too often the geometric part of Bock's sculpture is described in crudely Freudian terms as nothing more than phallic.

[18]Arthur Schopenhauer, *The World as Will and Representation*, vol. I [1819] (Dover reprint, New York, 1966), p. 129.

[19]The photograph Wright published in 1908 at the end of his first "In the Cause of Architecture" essay, and again in the 1910 *Ausgeführte Bauten von Frank Lloyd Wright*, was of a plaster cast, more crisp than the terra-cotta sculpture cast for the house by the Gates Company, the maker of Teco art pottery. Many early views by the Chicago Architectural Photographing Co. of the garden at Taliesin, the home and studio Wright began to build in 1911 near Spring Green, Wis., also show a plaster cast of the sculpture, later broken.

Neil Levine discusses the sculpture in "Frank Lloyd Wright's Own Houses and His Changing Concept of Representation," in *The Nature of Frank Lloyd Wright*, ed. Carol R. Bolon *et al.* (Chicago, 1988), p. 30. For a more elaborate and esoteric interpretation, see Narciso G. Menocal, "Taliesin, the Gilmore House and the *Flower in the Crannied Wall*," in *Wright Studies*, vol. I (Carbondale, Ill., 1992), pp. 70–80.

[20]In a succinct analysis of picturesque American shingled houses, A. D. F. Hamlin writes of the irregular plan and roof configuration, the frank expression of the plan in the exterior, ample piazzas (verandas) and "the enlargement of the entrance hall with its stairs into a living hall with fireplace"; see "The Genesis of the American Country House," the *Architectural Record XLII* (Oct. 1917), p. 298. Vincent Scully, Jr., discusses the same themes in *The Shingle Style* (New Haven, Ct., 1955), passim.

74. *Living hall, looking northeast.*

75. *Living-hall inglenook, looking northwest.*

76. *Fireplace, with Teco vase.*

Only the majestic inglenook can anchor the space [75]. The firedogs respond to the spire of the "Flower in the Crannied Wall," the arch of the fireplace echoes that of the entrance, and even the small gray floor tiles answer to the larger red tiles of the vestibule and entry. Wright's touch is everywhere: in the brickwork, the firescreen and firedogs, the tall-back settles and the special Teco vase ornamented with abstractions of sumac [76].[21] A true work of art, he said, ought not to be compromised:

> . . . it is quite impossible to consider the building one thing and its furnishings another . . .. They are all mere structural details of its character and completeness.[22]

Nothing so expresses his straight-line program of reform as the massive oak settles, conceived not for comfort but for rectitude—the corrective to Victorian furniture and all its sentimentality.

Even more austere, the living-room fireplace appears spare indeed [77]. The chimney mass, more than nine feet wide, nevertheless forms the foil to every other side of the room. Broad alcoves expand the space at the north and south walls to the full width of the old villa [78].[23] Standing brass lamps

[21]The oak furniture in the house is thought to have been made by the John W. Ayers Co., of Chicago; see David A. Hanks, *The Decorative Designs of Frank Lloyd Wright* (New York, 1979), pp. 201–202. The inglenook settles are 51 inches tall and 59 inches wide. A smaller settle stands below the stationary window to the living room. The special Teco vase measures about 231/2 inches tall and 111/2 inches at the base, and is stamped with shape no. 329. Also see Sharon S. Darling, *Teco: Art Pottery of the Prairie School* (Erie, Pa., 1989), p. 151. Although he designed several other Teco vases, Wright was not pleased with American art pottery. "We seem to have little or nothing to say in the clay figure or pottery vase as concrete expression of the ideal of beauty that is our own," he wrote in "In the Cause of Architecture: The Meaning of Materials—the Kiln," the *Architectural Record LXIII* (June 1928), p. 561.

[22]*Ausgeführte Bauten und Entwürfe von Frank Lloyd Wright*, n.p. In his 1901 lecture on "The Art and Craft of the Machine" Wright deplored "elaborate and fussy joinery of posts, spindles, jig sawed beams and braces, butted and strutted, to outdo the sentimentality of the already overwrought antique product."

[23]The north-south dimension is 28 feet, 4 inches—but only 18 feet 8 inches without the alcoves. The three-part alcove window groups resemble the so-called "Chicago window" of turn-of-the-century skyscrapers.

77. *Living room, looking predominantly west.*

78. *Living-room alcove, looking southwest.*

79. *Living-room lamp, north alcove.*

80. *Living-room bay, looking southeast.*

81. *Sitting room, looking northwest.*

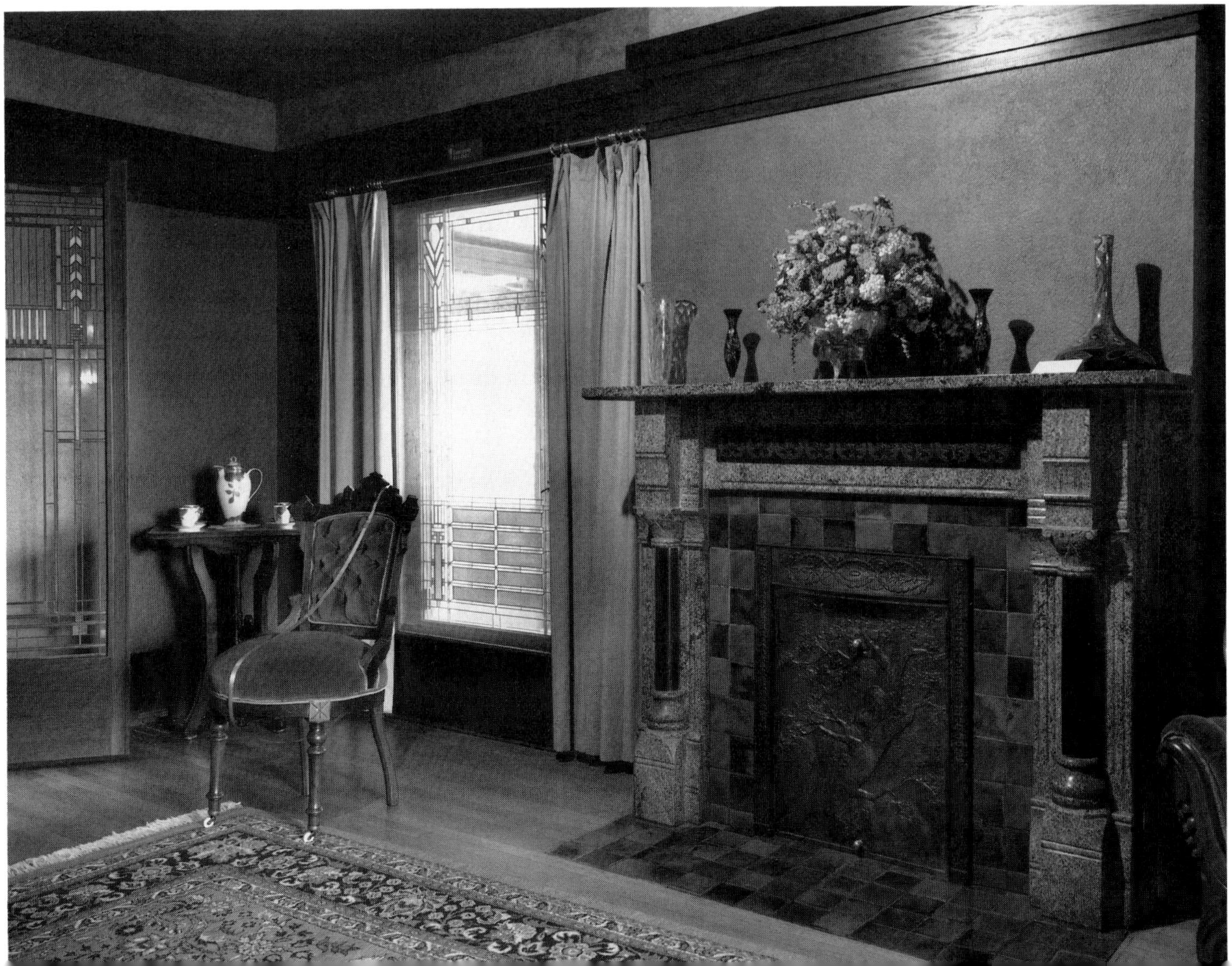

similar to those on the walls surmount the casepieces [79]. The ceiling rises from $6^1/_2$ feet at the doors and lateral alcoves to $10^1/_2$ feet in the central space. To the east, another alcove meets the morning light with a grand bay of art glass [80]. The library table, broad as the chimney mass, holds a double-pedestal bronze lamp with an art-glass shade.

The sitting room—or den, as it is called in a drawing for the glass doors—tenuously survives from the battle between Wright and the old villa [81]. Apart from the furniture, its single Victorian feature is the fireplace, with the carved butterflies; just enough, evidently, to satisfy Mrs. Dana and her yearnings for some sign of permanence at a site where three successive houses had been built in only three generations. The room itself has been wholly transformed by the elimination of the wallpaper, the lowered ceiling and the introduction of eight art-glass doors, three wall-mounted lamps and a stationary window to the living room. The doors to adjacent rooms are so inconspicuous that even when the portieres are open the sitting room remains largely hidden [82, 83].

Although the den opens to the dining room, the primary approach is clearly through the westward arm of the living hall, a carefully staged passage with dramatic changes in ceiling heights. From the central hall, which rises about 20 feet, the westward passage falls to 7 feet 4 inches; and the entrance to the dining room (like those to the living room, sitting room and breakfast alcove) descends to $6^1/_2$ feet [84]. But the vault of the dining room leaps almost as high as the living hall [85]. Even though it conforms to the distance that once separated the old villa from the summer kitchen, only $16^1/_2$ feet, the plan of the dining room suggests a basilica—with a vaulted nave, a low apse (the breakfast alcove) and the semblance, at least, of side aisles. The light stays low, thus quieting the richly ornamental details in the presence of

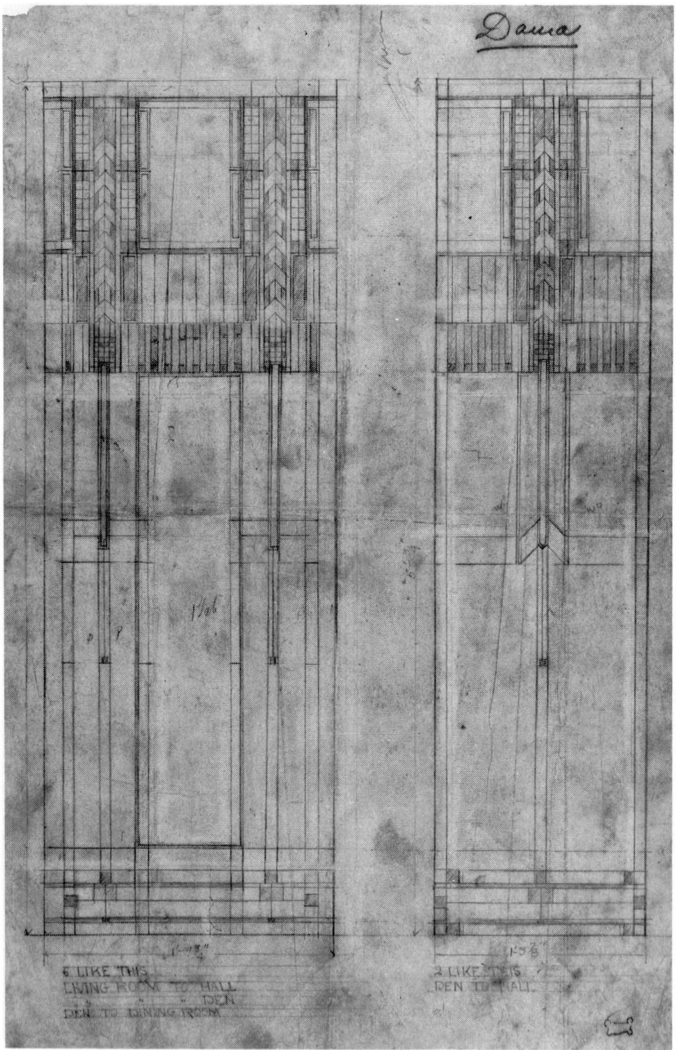

82. *Drawing for doors, den and living room.*

83. *Doors from den to living hall.*

84. *Entranceway to dining room, looking north.*

the tallback chairs and oak sideboard, so unyielding and reformist in spirit.

Some drawings show a long skylight above the dining table, but Wright evidently decided not to disturb the integrity of the vault or the quick rhythm of the ribs, only $27^1/_2$ inches from center to center [86]. Yet he was eager to interrupt the lunette. Charles E. White, Jr., told why:

> In this day of steel, he uses the arch very rarely and recognizes the lintel construction, by strong horizontal lines throughout the building. He is so adverse to the arch, that in a barrel vaulted room, he usually tries to eradicate the effect of the sloping lines of the tympanum, by horizontal architectural lines in the decoration, or trim. He enjoys the soffit of the vault, but dislikes the tympanum.[24]

So the curve of the lunette is effectively canceled by a post-and-lintel structure to carry portieres, as if they were needed for privacy [87].[25] Because the diago-

[24]"Letters, 1903–1906, by Charles E. White, Jr.," p. 106.

[25]Set far back on its site and nearly 50 feet away, the Stuart Brown house hardly threatened the privacy of the dining room. The three-story brick building now immediately north of the Dana house was constructed 35 years later, after the Brown house had been demolished.

85. *Dining-room vault, looking south.*

86. *Vault, looking northwest.*

87. *Lunette, looking north.*

nal lines of the art glass can suggest the gabled roof, the traditional principles of architectural structure again appear all at once. The glass design nevertheless professes to be an abstraction of sumac—diminutive and gregarious trees remarkable only in the fall, when their lance-shaped leaflets turn scarlet. Sumac is a spindly plant with drooping branches, but Wright conceived a forceful abstraction to transform it into a seminal motif [88]:

> The differentiation of a single, certain simple form characterizes the expression of one building. Quite a different form may serve for another . . . its grammar may be deduced from some plant form that has appealed to me, as certain properties in line and form of the sumach were used in the Lawrence house at Springfield . . ..[26]

Below the lunette, however, the dining-room frieze represents sumac in a straightforward if lyrical transcription, plainly the work of a different sensibility [89]. Wright's description is brief:

> The decorative frieze around the room is treated with the Shumac, Golden Rod, and Purple Aster that characterize our roadsides in September.[27]

The frieze sings a gentle hymn to the landscape in a room sequestered from the outdoors. It was painted

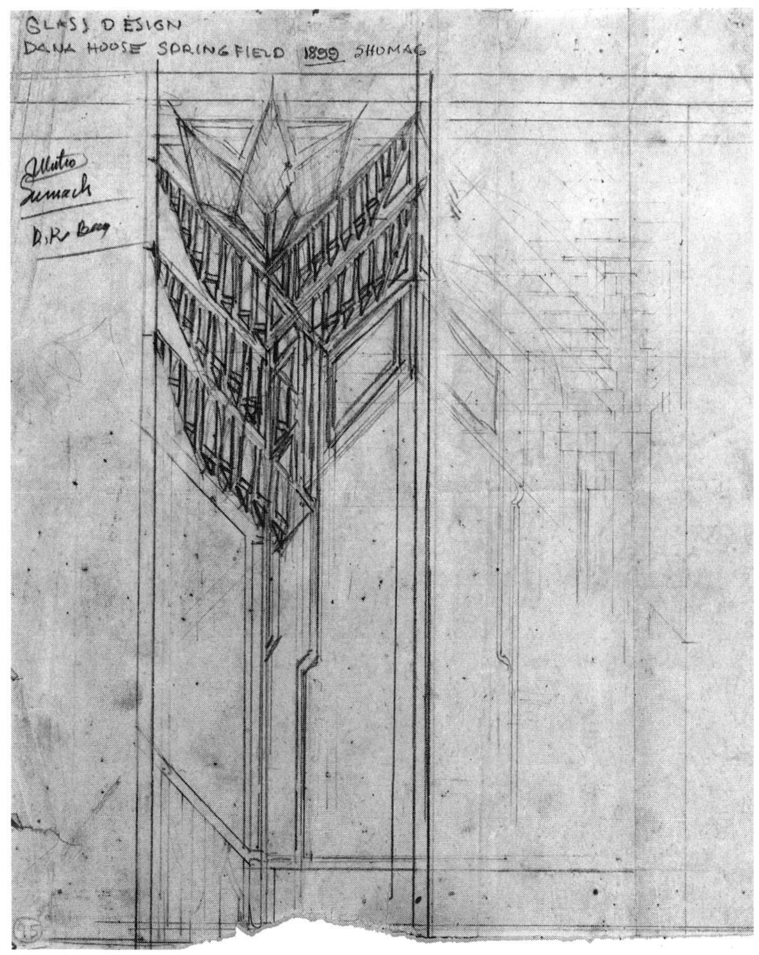

88. *Study for sumac pattern in breakfast alcove.*

[26]Wright, "In the Cause of Architecture," p. 161. Goethe defined a plant as a living structure that is a model of everything artistic.

[27]Wright, "In the Cause of Architecture," p. 211. The frieze panels are about forty inches tall.

89. *Frieze, looking north.*

into the sand-finish plaster by George M. Niedecken, who like Bock sometimes worked in the Oak Park studio. Niedecken's preliminary studies reveal an attention to nature that Wright normally would have dismissed as slavish imitation [90, 91].[28] By con-

[28]George Mann Niedecken (1878–1945) was an interior architect who had exhibited with the Chicago Arts and Crafts Society in 1898 at the eleventh annual Chicago Architectural Club exhibition. He was only 25 when Charles E. White, Jr., wrote early in 1904 that Niedecken had returned for a few days a week in the Oak Park studio. Niedecken also may have done the color presentation drawings of the Dana house. Those of the dining room show that a painted wood-panel screen to conceal the pantry door once was contemplated. Niedecken painted another sumac mural to flank the living-room fireplace of the Edward P. Irving house of 1909–11 in Decatur, Ill., designed by Wright but completed by Hermann V. von Holst with Marion Mahony. He also painted murals for the Avery Coonley house of 1907–09 in Riverside, Ill., and the Meyer May house of 1908–09 in Grand Rapids, Mich. See Cheryl Robertson and Terrence Marvel, *The Domestic Scene* (1897–1927): *George M. Niedecken, Interior Architect* (Milwaukee, Wis., 1981), passim.

Wright vigorously distinguished interpretation of nature from imitation of nature; his interest lay in the pattern of structure and articulation, not in semblance. An architect should rise "far above the realistic in his art," he wrote in "In the Cause of Architecture," p. 155.

90. *Niedecken's study for frieze of maple leaves and sumac.*

91. *Niedecken's study for frieze of sumac, goldenrods and asters.*

97. *Serving pantry.*

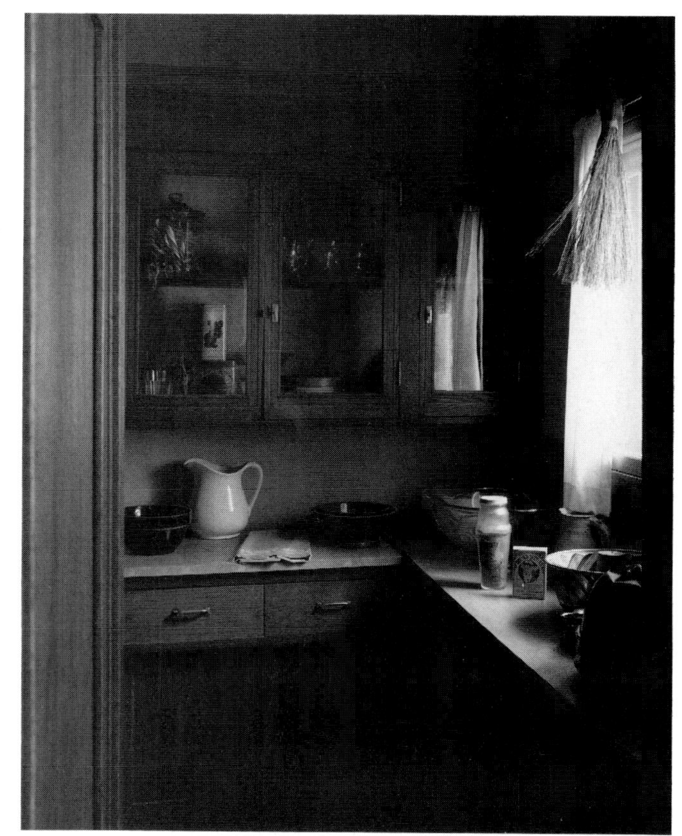

99. *Pantry and refrigerator room.*

98. *Kitchen, looking east.*

100. *Bedroom for Mrs. Lawrence, looking south.*

and alcove share a continuous glass screen of seven casements and transoms, and even the bathroom has an art-glass window onto the porch. The oak furniture speaks the language of reform [101, 102]. Or, as Wright declared in 1908:

> . . . furniture takes the clean cut, straight-line forms that the machine can render far better than would be possible by hand.[32]

But, in truth, everything calls for handcraft as well.

In the upper reaches of the living hall the russet, golden, green and brown hues of autumn are scumbled into the plaster surfaces with great care, not only to diversify the planes but to give them character and depth, thus life [103, 104]. Vases in hammered sheet copper hold dried weeds and flowers in homage to the prairie [105–107].[33] Other vessels and plaster statues assume their places on decks and posts to invigorate the space. A drawing for the central casements, which rise 10 feet, develops a pattern slightly altered in execution and then repeated for the tall windows of the studio [108]. If the design alludes to goldenrods, it nonetheless achieves an abstract clarity like that of an idealized ground plan.

[32]Wright, "In the Cause of Architecture," p. 162. He recommended built-in furniture even in 1894, when he said, "Too many houses are like notion stores, bazaars, and junk shops"; see *Frank Lloyd Wright: Collected Writings*, vol. 1, p. 24.

[33]The copper urn and vase evidently derived from an unusually clumsy design for two weed holders rising from a sphere. The urns, 18 inches in diameter, first appeared in Wright's own studio of 1898, then in an 1899 remodeling of the E. C. Waller house in River Forest, Ill., and possibly in the Husser house of 1899–1900. The design for those in the Dana house was slightly simplified and improved. The weed holders, about 28 inches tall, had appeared in Wright's home and studio, and possibly in the Isidore Heller house a year or two after it was built. The vessels were made by James A. Miller and Brother, of Chicago; see Hanks, *The Decorative Designs of Frank Lloyd Wright*, pp. 212–213.

It should be noted from the early photographs of the Dana house that despite the extraordinary level of Wright's sensibility, Mrs. Dana brought in the most common clay pots for flowers and positioned them conspicuously.

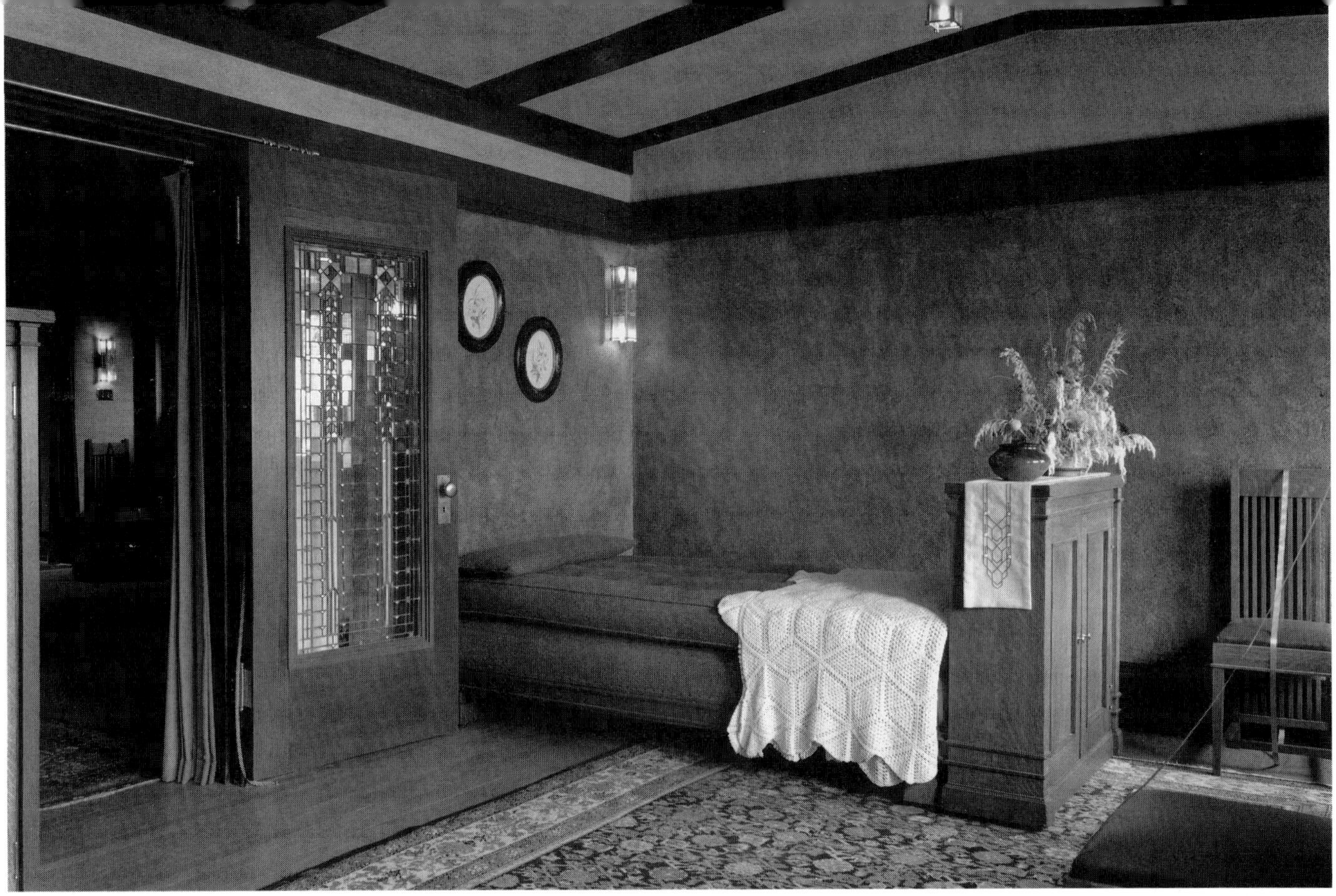

101. *Bedroom, looking northeast.*

102. *Bedroom, looking northwest.*

103. *Early view of living hall, looking southwest.*

104. *Early view of gallery level, looking predominantly south.*

105. *Sketch for copper urn 18 inches in diameter.*

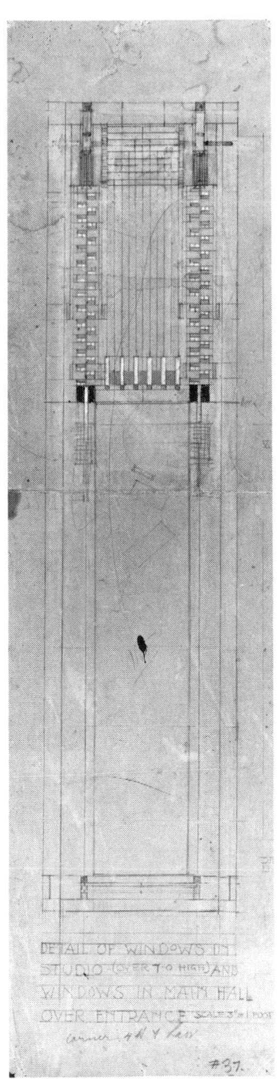

108. *Drawing for tall windows.*

106. *Copper urn.*

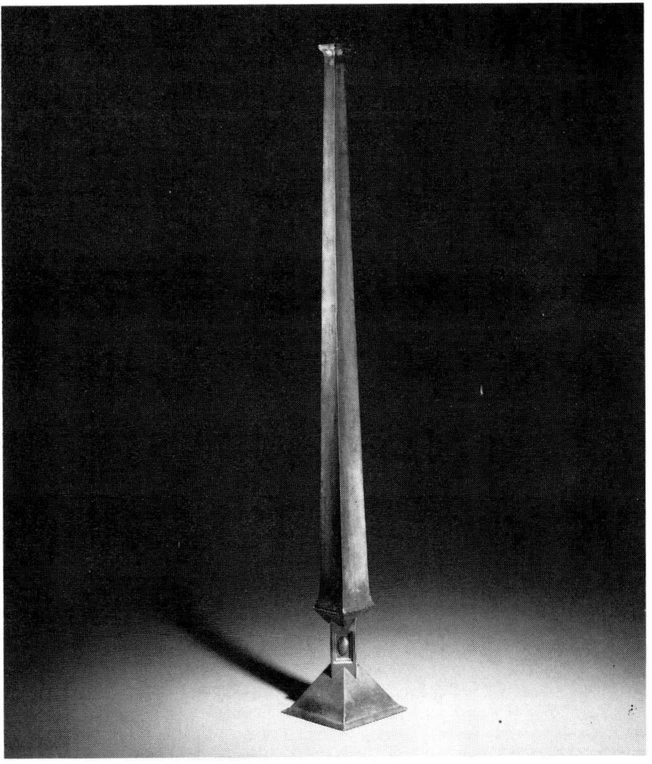

107. *Copper weed holder.*

112. *Master bedroom, looking west.*

twin beds are screened on all sides by portieres and matched by oversized dressing tables that obstruct most of the space in the rest of the room. The fireplace is again austere [112]. And again it counters an alcove at the east wall, where an astonishing bay of art glass rises as a continuation of the pattern in the windows below [113, 114]. Motifs inspired by staghorn sumac somehow metamorphose into a colossal butterfly, or perhaps a dragonfly. The house once more evokes the romance of flight.[35]

A door opens from the master bedroom to a small dressing area, and mirrored cabinets extend into the bathroom. In turn, this space opens to a small room probably intended as a nursery. It shares in the series of art-glass casements along the north wall. Four steps down, the hall that overlooks the dining room leads to the service wing, where stairs descend to the pantry and other steps rise to the servants' bedrooms and bathroom, all places of little note.[36] The suite for cousin Flora Lawrence, four steps up from the gallery, comprises a well-lighted bedroom with a built-in seat, a bathroom and a dressing room with mirrored wardrobes [115, 116]. The small loggia opens to the south but offers a more engaging vista westward, toward the studio lunette [117].

[35]Wright's abstraction should be contrasted with the realism of the popular Tiffany dragonfly lamp shades of the period 1899–1915.

[36]The hall could serve as a musicians' balcony for entertaining dinner guests. The north servant's room is only slightly larger than the nursery, and the other servant's room is smaller than the nursery. Both rooms have awkward access through the bathroom to the balcony, where the tall brick parapet, unrelieved by openings, blocks summer breezes.

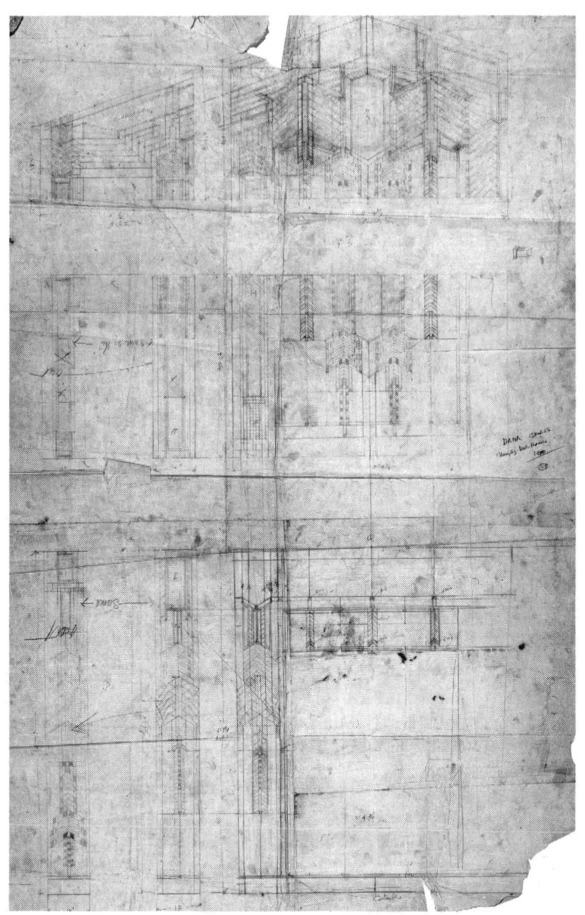

113. *Drawing for window ensemble, living room and master bedroom.*

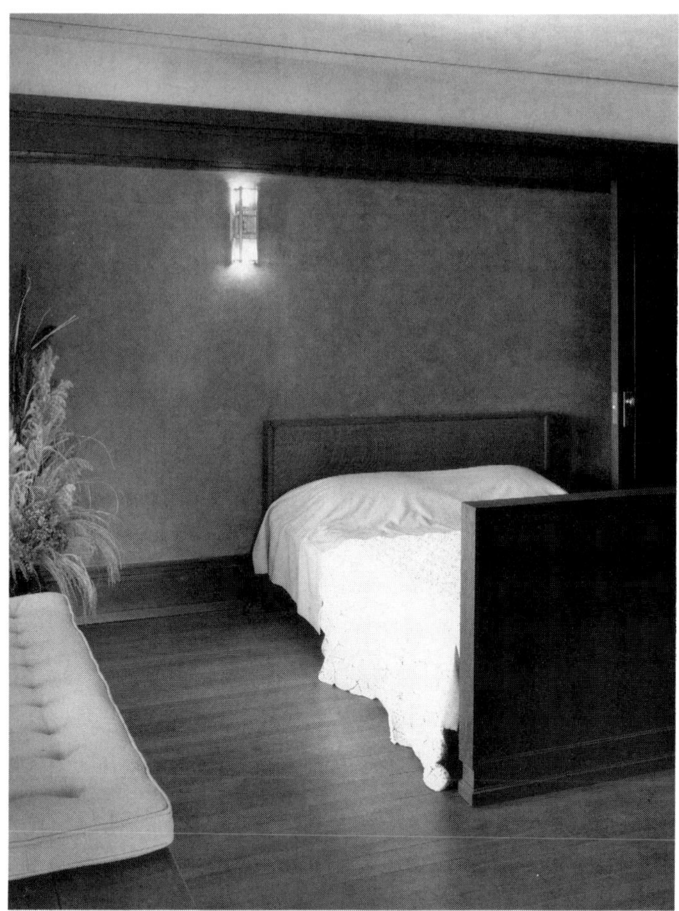

115. *West bedroom, looking predominantly north.*

114. *Master bedroom, looking east.*

116. *Dressing room, looking east.*

117. *Loggia, looking west.*

To the Studio

A SINGLE DRAWING can illustrate the wonderfully controlled complexity of the Dana house [118]. How the main house relates to the garden court and studio, for instance, is far from obvious. Early studies of the living hall showed little more than a library table and chairs by a broad opening to the court [119]. Later, to screen a passage from the kitchen to the studio, the scheme grew subtle.

The service passage is defined by a resplendent series of art-glass doors and windows behind a sculptural fountain [120]. Although the glass shimmers with the afternoon sun, the fountain stays shrouded in darkness. Its theme is the moon. Hence it refers to the lunettes of the dining room and studio, the rooms between which it in fact mediates. To encircle the source, a water jar round as the moon, Bock conceived sensuous nude figures [121, 122]:

> There was another piece of sculpture for the Dana House which awaited completion. It had been started by Marion Mahony from a sketch I had made . . . [of] a rising full moon filled with happy children's figures. Miss Mahony's splendid interpretation of this

118. *Transverse section, looking west.*

119. *Living hall, study for presentation drawing.*

120. *Glass screen behind fountain.*

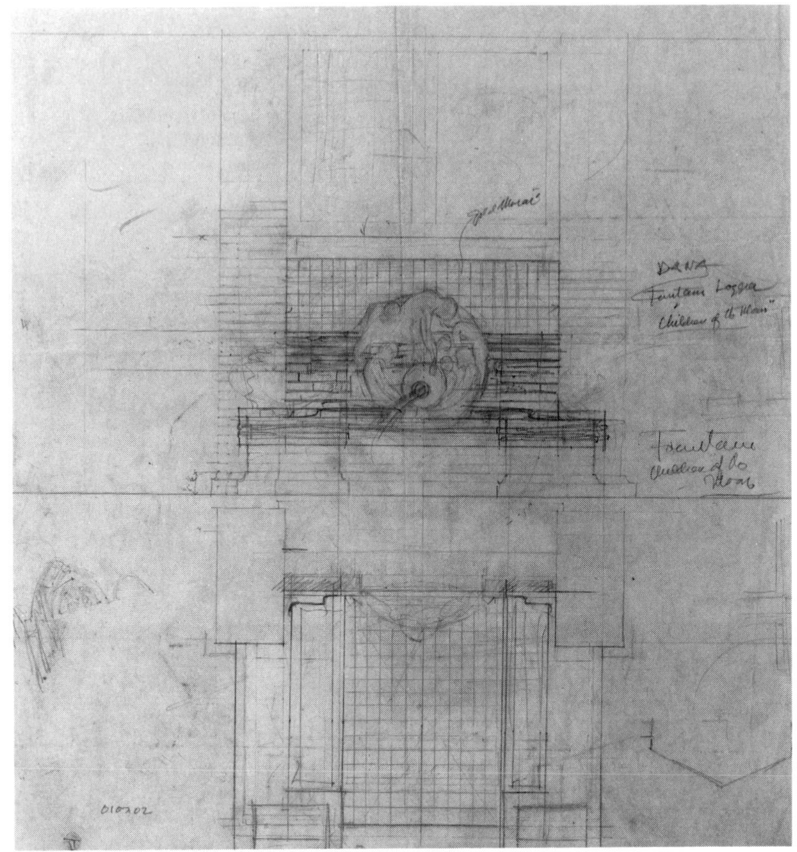

121. *Sketch for fountain; elevation and plan.*

122. *"The Moon Children," lighted.*

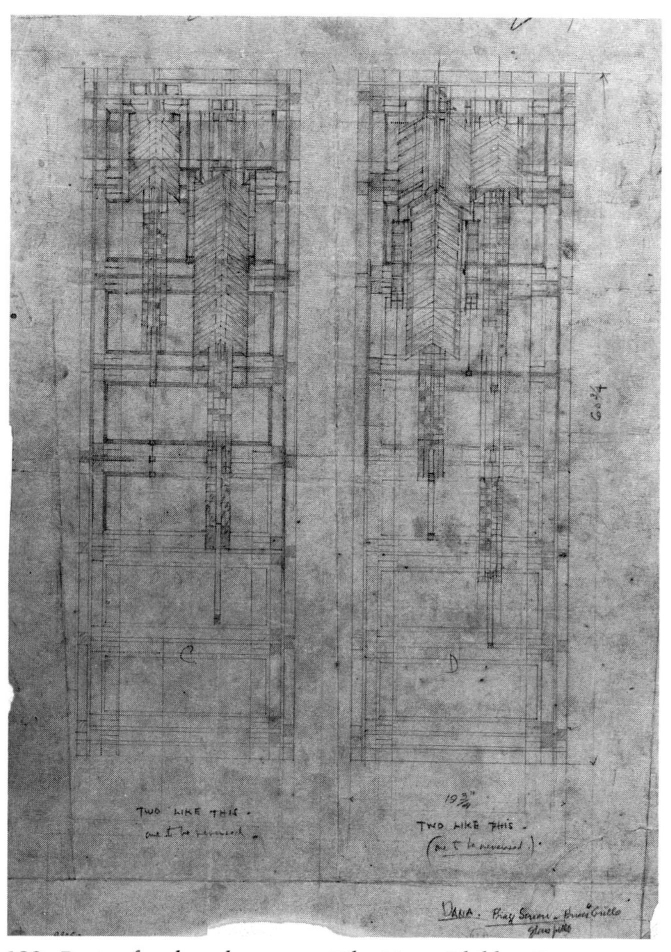

123. *Design for glass doors near "The Moon Children."*

124. *Glass pattern in doors near fountain.*

125. *Glass patterns above fountain.*

small sketch was to be used as a wall fountain . . . and needed a lot more work for completion. I called this fountain "The Moon Children". . ..[1]

By evoking moonlight so close to the sunny garden court, Wright declared his affection for subdued interior light, and again he subverted the curved shape of the moon by imposing the horizontal, this time in the form of stratified clouds in sympathy with the prairie landscape.[2]

Many years later, Wright remembered the doors and windows behind the fountain as the "finest of all" his glass designs [123–125].[3] The patterns defy

126. *Hall behind fountain, looking south.*

[1]Bock, *Memoirs of an American Artist*, p. 82. Marion Mahony was still at work on the fountain as late as May 1904. Bock was working on lunettes, oddly, at the Schiller Theater in Chicago when he first met Wright. "Moon Children" was cast in terra-cotta by the William D. Gates Co.

[2]Peisch, in *The Chicago School of Architecture*, p. 49, writes that "Wright's developments in the field of interior lighting were influenced by what he referred to in conversation as 'moonlight.'" In examining an unusually bright photograph of the fountain, Wright was spurred to apply a soft pencil to the image to shade over the terra-cotta and brickwork. Stratified clouds—probably inspired as well by Japanese woodblock prints—appeared earlier in the playroom mural of his Oak Park home and in the rendering of "A Home in a Prairie Town." The fountain advances 4 feet into the living hall and is $5^1/_2$ feet wide.

[3]Wright, letter of Feb. 24, 1951, to Charles C. Thomas. All the art-glass work was by the Linden Glass Co. of Chicago; as to the cost, Wright recalled in a letter of Jan. 25, 1950 to Thomas: "Linden Glass contract about $15,000.00 or less." Frank L. Linden was a member of the Chicago Architectural Club. In 1889 he frescoed the clubroom walls with tints of gray and lavender, the *Inland Architect* reported.

127. *Vista into garden court, looking west, 1955.*

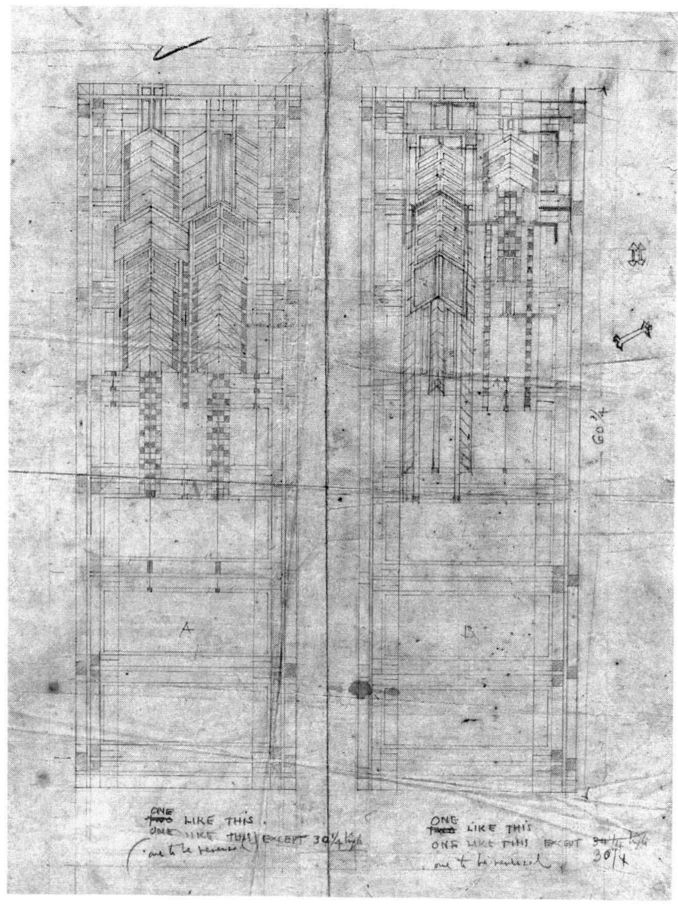

128. *Glass design for doors to corridor.*

129. *Glass pattern in doors to corridor.*

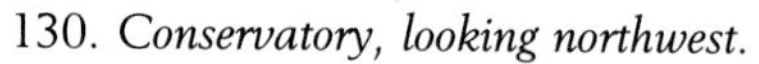

130. *Conservatory, looking northwest.*

131. *Doors to porch, looking southwest.*

literal interpretation because they allude to such various sources: the leaflets of sumac, the gables of the roof, wisteria trailing from latticework.[4]

The passage behind the fountain and glass screen opens to the garden court [126, 127]. It also leads to the studio; but the direct way from the living hall is through glass doors of yet another pattern [128, 129]. They open to the corridor and conservatory, composed of seven bays of paired casement windows with art-glass ceiling lights below a continuous skylight [130].[5] Opposite the conservatory, the glass doors give to the porch, from which guests can arrive [131]. A large stationary window at the west wall of the porch overlooks the stairwell to the li-

[4]For the Helen Husser house, Wright had collaborated with Blanche Ostertag, a painter, illustrator and decorative artist, to design a fireplace mosaic that Spencer described in *The Work of Frank Lloyd Wright*, p. 72, as "a weeping profusion of wisteria sprays and pendant blossoms upon a ground dull gold below and bright gold above a suggested horizon." Irma Strauss suggests that the mosaic may never have been installed; see the *Frank Lloyd Wright Newsletter*, vol. 2, no. 1 (1979), p. 6n. Wisteria mosaics by Orlando Giannini surrounded the double fireplace of Wright's house of 1904–06 for Darwin D. Martin, in Buffalo, N.Y.

[5]The rhythm of bays, spaced 6 feet center to center, does not express any module for the rest of the house; the posts of the living-hall gallery, for instance, are spaced slightly more than 5 feet apart.

132. *Porch, looking predominantly west.*

133. *South terrace, looking west.*

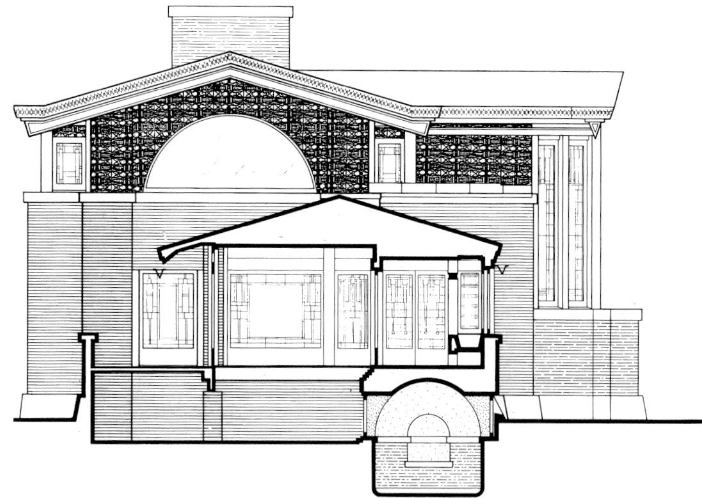

134. *Transverse section through porch and corridor, looking west.*

brary, and the adjacent door provides access to either the library or the studio [132]. Screen doors address the south terrace, which continues east and passes the windows of the bedroom suite [133].

Although an early study envisions an arched passage at the west end of the corridor, the arch instead appears as the vaulted ceiling of the bowling alley, as shown by a transverse section [134]. The glass doors from the corridor to the studio are again of a different pattern [135]. A vintage photograph documents the elegance of the original portieres [136]. Past the doorway, an unexpected opening between brick piers creates a bewildering vista into the library stairwell, a space that never fails to stir the imagination [137].

The way to the studio turns three times within a crystalline bay, a great passage of the house [138–140]. Its effect—so characteristic of Wright—is to forestall arrival and thereby exalt the destination. Two perspective studies and a presentation drawing indicate that Wright grasped the idea of the studio quickly and firmly [141–143]. The presentation drawing offers the clue; it bears the motto "Life is Truth" above the inglenook fireplace, a studied in-

135. *Corridor, looking west.*

136. *Doors to studio, with original portieres.*

137. *Vista into library stairwell, looking south.*

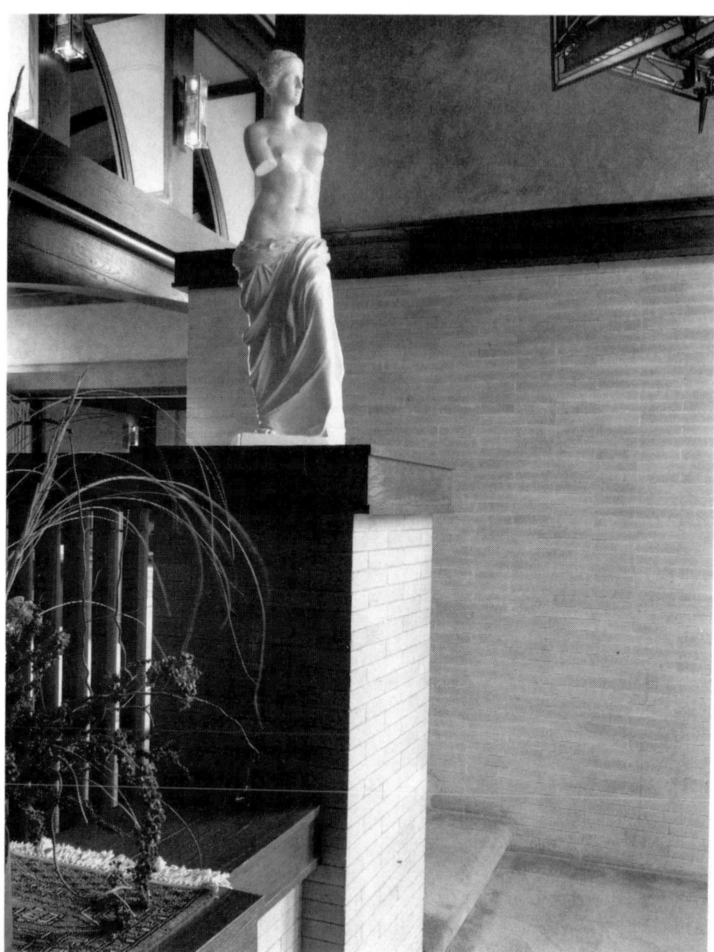

138. *Stair landing to studio, looking predominantly west.*

139. *Stair landing, looking north.*

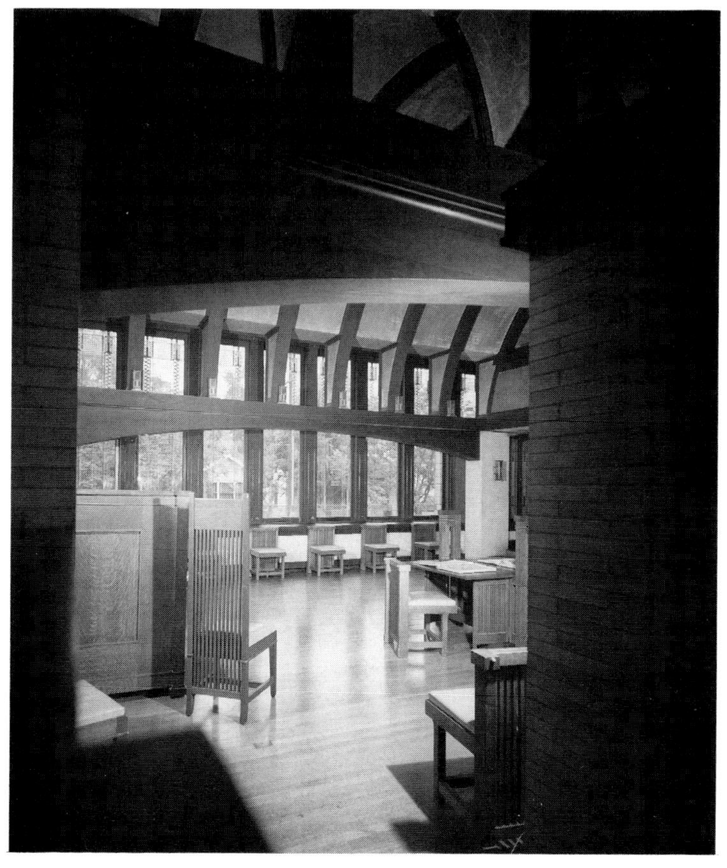

140. *Vista into studio, looking predominantly south.*

141. *Study for presentation drawing of studio, looking southwest.*

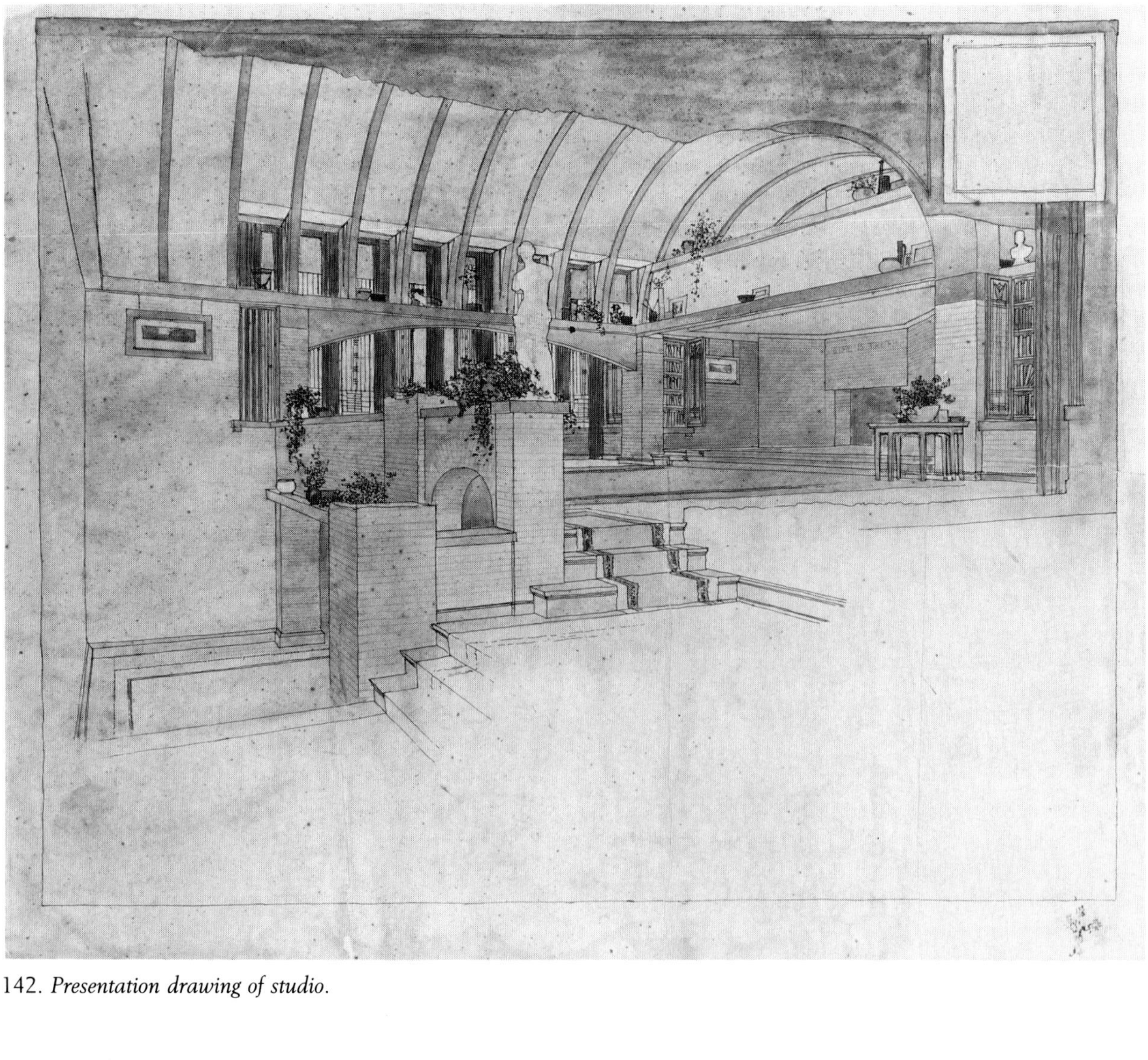

142. *Presentation drawing of studio.*

143. *Study for west end of studio.*

version of the words "Truth is Life" carved at the inglenook of Wright's own home.[6] He had simply conceived the studio as a more refined variation of his Oak Park playroom [144]. John Lloyd Wright recalled how much the playroom meant to the life of the house:

> My first impression upon coming into the playroom from the narrow, long, low-arched, dimly lighted

[6] Another drawing for the Dana house specified a "motto carved on mantel shelf" at the living-room fireplace. It, too, was left unexecuted. Wright's fondness for mottoes accompanied his spirit of reform. He used them in the Oak Park studio, the Hillside Home School, the William R. Heath house and especially the Larkin Building.

Often called the "gallery," the studio is neither a formal art gallery nor an enclosed passageway. It was consistently identified as the studio in the working drawings and in early accounts of social events at the house, and was remembered by Wright as the studio when he annotated the drawing reproduced here as Fig. 141 and when he annotated a photograph taken by Maynard Parker in 1955.

144. *Oak Park playroom of 1895, with genie mural; looking east.*

145. *Studio, looking northeast.*

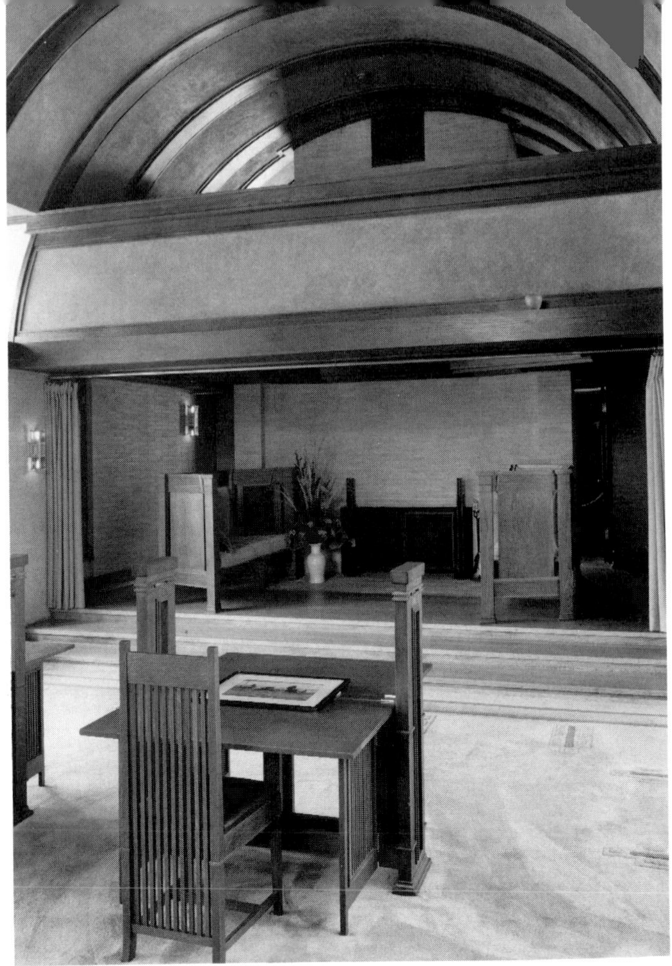

146. *Studio, looking predominantly west.*

passageway that led to it was its great height and brilliant light . . .. In this room were the milestones to maturity; treasures, friends, comrades, ambitions; and through the years I have dreamed through the inspiration of this playroom.[7]

In the studio the ribs of the vault spring from long shelves with rows of standing art-glass lamps [145]. Beneath the shelves, attenuated arches opposite to those of the vault broadly frame the narrow alcoves. The central space, nearly square, is cunningly shielded from the railroad by the inglenook and balcony [146]. Two special tables display Japanese woodblock prints.[8] The tallback inglenook settles are angled like the fireplace mass and the ceiling light; all may allude to butterflies [147].

An early photograph of the studio records Mrs. Dana's fondness for ferns and flowers and Indian pottery [148]. The item most at odds with the scale of the room and with Wright's sensibility, however, is the freestanding music cabinet [149]. Its fussy glass

[7]John Lloyd Wright, *My Father Who Is on Earth*, pp. 16–17. The studio of the Dana house is essentially an adult playroom.

[8]Similar print tables were made for Wright's home and studio and for the Francis W. Little house in Peoria, Ill.

147. *Studio inglenook, looking west.*

148. *Early view of studio, looking predominantly south.*

design and clumsy proportions speak of office work, perhaps by Marion Mahony or even George Niedecken.[9] By contrast, the grand settle, which has shelves at the back, stands by the low parapet at the stairwell in quiet majesty [150].

A post-and-lintel structure crosses the lunette at the east end of the vault to support what Wright called the "suspended glass screen"—a tapestry of art glass unique in his work [151].[10] The nine panels of slender plantlike abstractions bring to mind the free-hand patterns he had drawn for the private edition of *The House Beautiful.* With the gable as a background, the frame once more conjoins all three of Ruskin's "good architectures" [152].

Two drawings illustrate the relation of the studio

[9]Niedecken in 1910 designed an equally awkward-looking music cabinet for the E. P. Irving house in Decatur, Ill.; see *The Domestic Scene* (1897–1927), p. 73.

[10]Wright, notation on a photograph taken in June 1955 by Maynard Parker. Strangely, the lunette is at the east wall, just as the tympanum mural of the genie is at the east wall of Wright's playroom of 1895; the early presentation drawing reproduced here as Fig. 35 shows the lunette ornamented by a winged figure reminiscent of the genie.

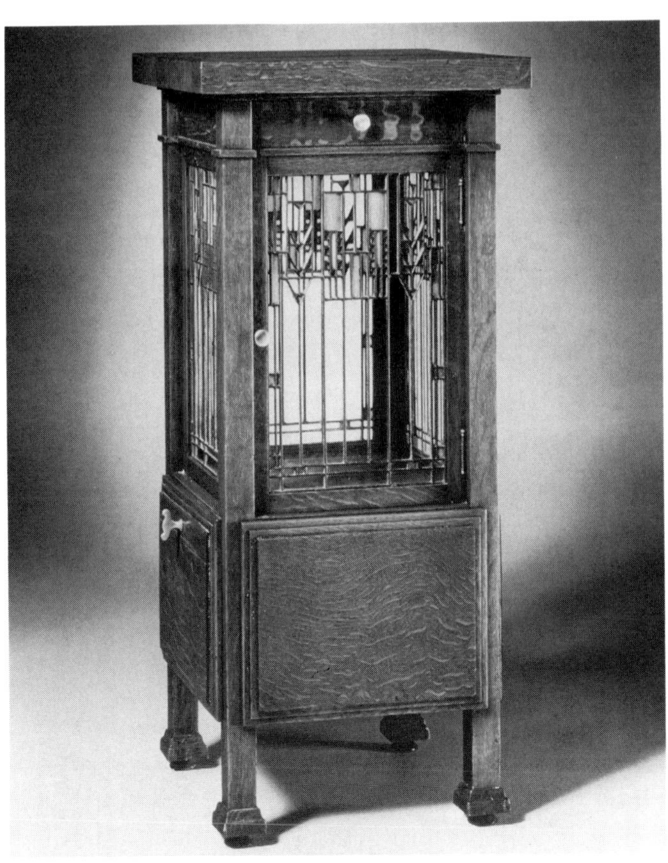

149. *Music cabinet.*

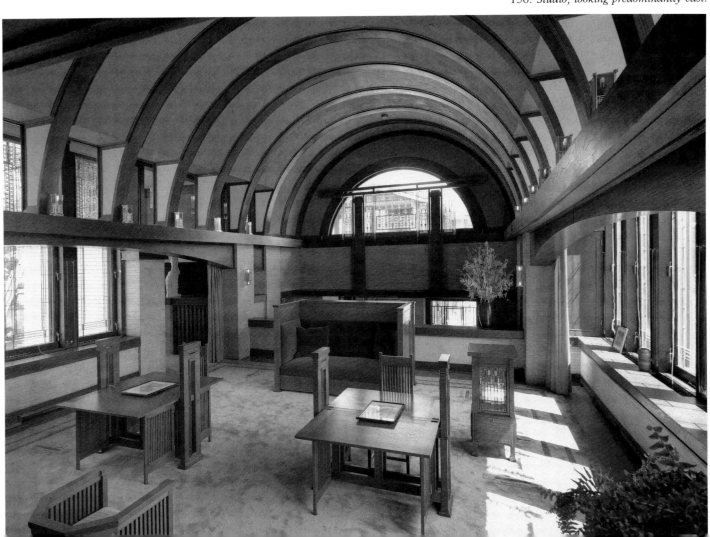

150. *Studio, looking predominantly east.*

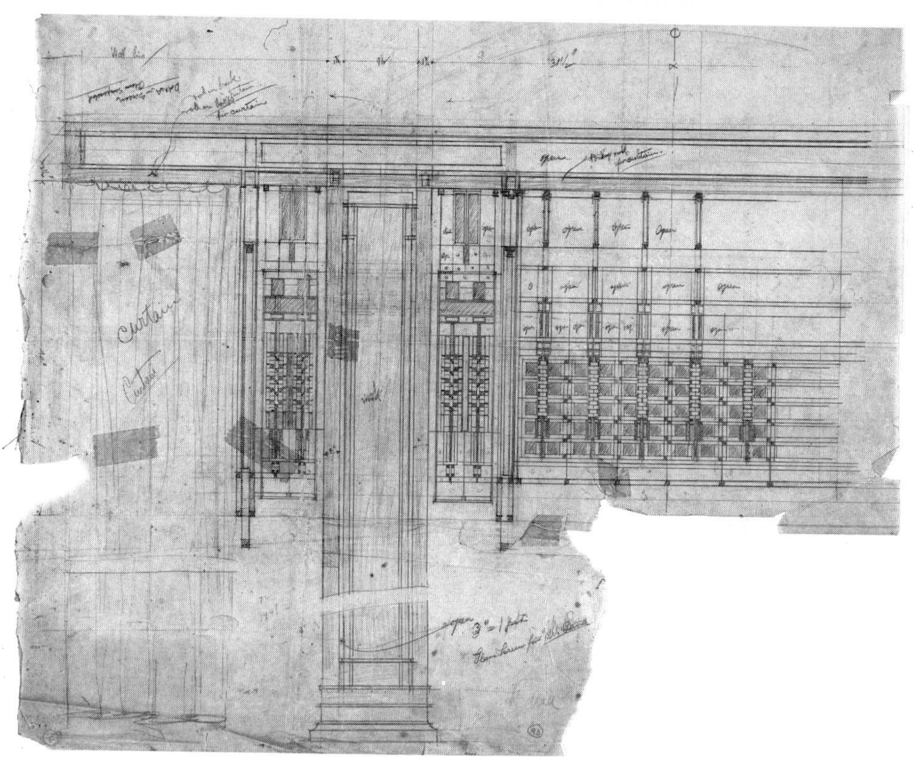

151. *Design for glass screen.*

152. *Glass screen, looking predominantly east.*

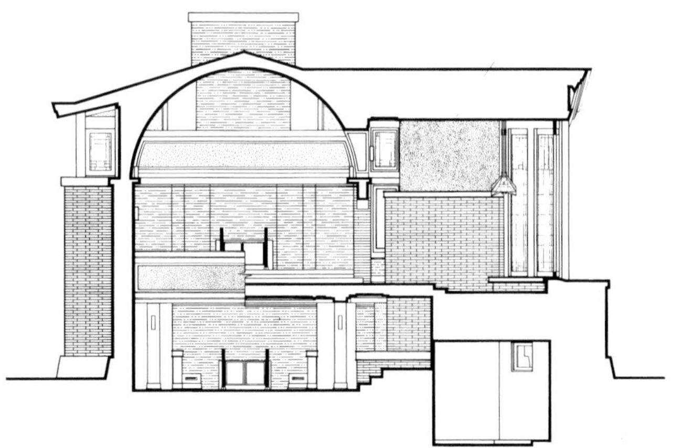

153. *Transverse section through studio and library, looking west.*

154. *Vista into library and studio; rendering of 1910.*

155. *Library stairwell, looking east.*

to the space of the library, originally designated a "waiting room" for social events upstairs [153, 154]. The library floor, clearly below grade, nevertheless finds the same level as the entry to the main house, 5 1/2 feet below the first story. Despite daylight from the stairwell and all the lamps along the book alcoves, the light remains dim [155, 156]. The table lamps with 16-sided shades glory in a radial symmetry like that of the purple asters of the prairie landscape.[11] Although the rendering from 1910 shows full-size armchairs, Mrs. Dana intended the library especially for children—as the little side chairs, only 29 inches tall, make evident. That her own sons had died in in-

[11]In addition to the table lamps, the library has 15 lamps mounted horizontally on beams and eight lamps mounted vertically on wood-finished piers. The stairwell functions much like the light-wells of early Chicago skyscrapers; the prismatic lights of the south terrace likewise demonstrate Wright's familiarity with commercial architecture.

156. *Library, looking southwest.*

157. *Inglenook, looking predominantly west.*

fancy gives the inglenook an inescapable melancholy [157].

The basement, six steps down from the library, offers different diversions, a vaulted duckpin alley and a vaulted room suitable for billiards [158, 159].[12] At the west side of the room a steel door guards a safety vault. The door is inscribed:

Rheuna D. Lawrence Estate
Mary Agnes Lawrence
Susan Lawrence Dana

[12]In 1907 a bowling lane appeared next to a billiard table on the lower level of an addition Wright designed for the Fox River Country Club, near Geneva, Ill.; see "George and Nelle Fabyan's Country Home," the *Frank Lloyd Wright Quarterly*, vol. 6 (Winter 1995), p. 7. Biltmore, the house of 1887–95 for George W. Vanderbilt in Asheville, N.C., has two bowling alleys, as well as a swimming pool, in its vast basement.

158. *Bowling alley, looking west.*

159. *Billiard room, looking south.*

No Other House That Compares

THE END OF 1904 found Frank Lloyd Wright listless and exhausted. Besides the strain of so much work in the Oak Park studio, he had become involved with the wife of a client. Everyone agreed it would be good for him to take a very long trip. And he did. In February 1905, together with his own wife and with Mr. and Mrs. Ward W. Willits, his clients for the first of the great prairie houses, he left for Japan. The day before Wright left, Charles E. White, Jr., wrote his friend in Vermont:

> There is no one at the Studio who appeals to me in the least, with the exception of young Byrne, and he is only a child. The rest of the bunch are interested strictly in their own affairs. The one thing they need above all else there is the French "esprit de corps," instead of each one pulling in an opposite direction. Of course they are all exceedingly friendly, but you feel it comes from the lips instead of from the heart . . .. I am glad your trip did you much good . . .. It is precisely this lack of attention to a vacation that has caused Mr. Wright to become so sort of petered out this last year. For the past three months it has been almost impossible to get him to give any attention to us. As he expresses it, he "has no appetite for work," and I think the reason is that he has taken no period of complete rest from his work in several years.[1]

Mrs. Dana had asked Wright to design a library for the new Lawrence School, about ten blocks south of her new house.[2] The school was named for her father, and she donated the room immediately west of the main entrance as a further memorial. Given that the new building lacked any charm and he lacked any appetite for work, Wright must have regarded the commission as little more than routine [160]. The single sheet with the plan and elevations is notably dated March 7, 1905, three weeks after he had left for Japan.

That same winter, Mrs. Dana and her mother took a long trip. They traveled to the Bahamas, then returned to Palm Beach and Jacksonville, Florida. They were on a train to Savannah, Georgia, when, on March 11, Mrs. Lawrence suffered a heart attack and died at 64.[3] Having lost her sons, her husband, her

[1]"Letters, 1903–1906, by Charles E. White, Jr.," p. 109.

[2]Historians for many years assumed that the "Lawrence Memorial Library" was the room below the studio, thus believed that the studio wing had been added to the Dana house. The two rooms have the same orientation and are about the same size; the library at the school—reconstructed in 1991–92 from funds raised by a citizen's committee—measures about 25 feet north–south and 30 feet east–west, and the Dana house library measures 24½ feet north–south and about 31 feet from the face of the fireplace to the open stairwell at the east.

The library at the school was rediscovered by state historians after the Dana house was purchased for the public; see James Allen, John Patterson and Richard Taylor, "Frank Lloyd Wright and Springfield's Lawrence School," *Historic Illinois*, April 1982, pp. 2, 3, 12, 13.

[3]An obituary in the *Illinois State Journal*, March 13, 1905, p. 6 noted that the "elegant new residence of Mrs. Lawrence and her daughter, completed last fall, has been the scene of many functions given for charity during the winter."

Mrs. Lawrence left no will; again, Mrs. Dana became administrator of the estate, as well as the sole heir. The probate record (no. 6478) states that after paying expenses she inherited $5733.72 from her mother.

160. *Lawrence Memorial Library, in the Lawrence School.*

father, all her grandparents and now her mother, Mrs. Dana resumed her queries to the spirit world. To her mother and father:

> Will I ever get anything out of the mines? If so, which ones? Must I sell the house or any of the other property?

And to her father:

> What will be my great mission in life—what field will fill the great big craving of my heart—
>
> I crave knowledge, wisdom and money—surely God will grant them to me—when I only want them for the good I can do humanity with them . . ..
>
> I am so worried because I did not insure Mamma's life—I need the money . . ..

Mrs. Dana needed money because she managed it so poorly. Her papers show that by 1915 the annual income from five of her father's rental properties approached $10,000; and by then she had borrowed $132,500 on six different notes. Only cousin Flora Lawrence survived in the household as a member of the family, but Mrs. Dana kept a cook, a maid and a coachman at the house and employed two other servants from nearby. Her entertainments made news. One day in June 1906 she held two receptions and a garden party. Musicians played from the living-hall landing, flowers surrounded the fountain, Japanese lanterns lit the court—it was described as "inconceivably pretty"—and guests could dance on a canopied platform.[4]

Wright visited Springfield two months earlier and as a guest of the Woman's Club spoke to a small audience at the Central Baptist Church. With regard to

[4]*Illinois State Journal*, June 23, 1906, p. 6. For a holiday party on Jan. 3, 1907, the house was described as having been "handsomely adorned with cut flowers and myriads of brilliant lights"; see the *Illinois State Journal*, Jan. 4, 1907, p. 6.

civic beautification, he said, the need for the landscape architect was greater than that for the architect.[5]

In April 1907, for the first time in five years, he took part in the annual exhibition of the Chicago Architectural Club at the Art Institute. Details from the Dana house were among his 38 exhibits [161]. Photographs of the house began to appear elsewhere that year, and by 1911 the house had been well published both nationally and abroad.[6]

But what made an impression in Springfield was Mrs. Dana's clandestine marriage to a concert baritone hardly half her age. She met Jörgen Constantin

[5]*Illinois State Journal*, Apr. 25, 1906, p. 4.

[6]See the *American Architect & Building News XCII*, part 1 (Aug. 24, 1907); the *Cyclopedia of Architecture, Carpentry and Building* (Chicago, 1907); "In the Cause of Architecture," the *Architectural Record*, vol. XXIII (March 1908); the *Architectural Review XV* (April 1908), and *Ausgeführte Bauten von Frank Lloyd Wright* (Berlin, 1910).

161. *Exhibit at the Art Institute of Chicago, 1907.*

Dahl, a native of Denmark, through a friend in Chicago, where he taught music, and they married on March 19, 1912, in Philadelphia. She was 49, and Dahl—who agreed to conflate her family name with his own, to become Lawrence Joergen-Dahl—was only 25. The marriage went unannounced in Springfield for more than two months. Not much more than a year later, in Chicago, young Joergen-Dahl died.[7] In 1915, after a third marriage, Mrs. Joergen-Dahl changed her name to Susan Lawrence-Gehrmann; more inclusively, she sometimes called herself Susan Lawrence Dana Joergen-Dahl Gehrmann. Her third and last husband, Charles A. Gehrmann, was a native of Springfield. At the time of their marriage she gave her age as 44 when in fact she was 52. Gehrmann was 51.[8]

Whatever name she used, Mrs. Lawrence-Gehrmann lived as she pleased, and espoused women's rights. Jane Addams of Hull-House had attended her reception for Chicago women who traveled to Springfield in 1909 to rally for suffrage legislation.[9] In 1923, on being named legislative chair for the Illinois branch of the National Woman's Party, Mrs. Lawrence-Gehrmann issued a statement:

> We mean to win for all women:
>
> Equal control of their children, equal control of their property, equal control of their earnings, equal right to make contracts, equal citizenship rights, equal inheritance rights, equal control of national, state and local government, equal opportunities in schools and universities, equal opportunities in government service, equal opportunities in professions and industries, equal pay for equal work, equal authority in the church, equal rights after their marriage to their own identity, and an equal moral standard. In short—equal rights with men in all laws and customs . . . .[10]

Mrs. Lawrence-Gehrmann at the same time continued her nebulous spiritual quests. Her library numbered hundreds of books on the occult, the mind, numerology, psychic healing and such. After three years of conducting what she called the "Springfield Society of Applied Psychology," she announced in 1924 that she would establish in her home the "Lawrence Metaphysical Center." In 1927 the enterprise was advertised as the "Lawrence Center of Constructive Thought," with classes offered in metaphysics, psychology and unity at a downtown center, the Lawrence Building.[11]

The move downtown probably testified to the fact that Mrs. Lawrence-Gehrmann, now living in greatly reduced circumstances, had quietly closed the grand house at Fourth and Lawrence. Cousin Flora Lawrence, very ill, had moved into the cottage across the tracks, at 231 East Lawrence Avenue. There she was cared for by Mrs. Lawrence-Gehrmann, who began to take her meals in a boardinghouse across the street. The other boarders, who worked at the state house, knew her as "Aunt Susie." Much later, one of them recalled that she took a taxi each year to St. Louis, 90 miles away, to buy gourmet supplies for their Christmas dinner.[12]

Cousin Flora Lawrence, so many years a presence at the homestead, died on May 27, 1928, two days before her seventy-fifth birthday.[13] That left Mrs. Lawrence-Gehrmann to live alone; she had been estranged from her husband many years. She divorced him in September 1930, then consulted a numerologist in New York and changed her name to Susan Z. Lawrence, as though she had never married.

Over the years, she kept in touch with Frank Lloyd Wright, not always happily. Their point of contention was the Hillside Home School, which had failed. Wright offered to discount her stock in the school corporation. She responded in December 1916:

> I am enclosing to you the note of the aunts and the stock.
>
> I of course do not know what your point of view brings to your mind in regard to the settling and adjusting of these matters with others than myself—their affairs were purely business matters, money advanced as lent for which they received security.
>
> I not only took stock but loaned the money without security. In addition gave the price of the building and the equipment in cash.

[7]The marriage was belatedly reported by the *Illinois State Register* on May 21, 1912, p. 1, which described Mrs. Dana as "a woman of wealth and social prominence in Springfield." Earlier that month Joergen-Dahl had sung in a musicale at the Dana house in honor of Gov. Charles Deneen and his wife. He died on July 26, 1913; see the *Illinois State Journal*, July 27, 1913, p. 8.

[8]Gehrmann's father, born in Germany, opened a dry-goods store in Springfield in 1861; see the *History of Sangamon County, Illinois*, p. 667. Gehrmann was born two years later.

[9]*Illinois State Journal*, Apr. 15, 1909, p. 6.

[10]*Illinois State Register*, Feb. 18, 1923, pp. 1, 10.

[11]*Illinois State Journal*, Aug. 3, 1924, part 3, p. 1, and Nov. 27, 1927, part 3, p. 4.

[12]"Clarence W. Klassen Memoir, Illinois Statecraft," Oral History office, Sangamon State University, 1984, pp. 29–30. The boardinghouse was operated by a widow and her daughter at 230 East Lawrence Avenue.

[13]See the obituary in the *Illinois State Register*, May 28, 1928, p. 2.

> After acting in the interests of the aunts at every turn, I hardly thought you would class me with the others, by offering me .50 [sic] percent.
>
> It hurt and surprised me—
>
> There is nothing to be realized out of the building. Under the circumstances, I feel I should have the face value of the note—and interest—or its equivalent. There is due $1,400 interest and $2,000 principal.
>
> The [Japanese] prints came tonight. I am going East in three weeks. I will take them to Boston and have Spaulding look them over and give me an estimate on them.
>
> We can then talk the matter over when you return [from Japan].

Wright probably had offered to satisfy part of the debt with woodblock prints, a practice he had begun soon after his first trip to Japan, almost 12 years earlier.[14]

When she wrote Wright in 1933 about visiting his studio-home in Wisconsin, Miss Lawrence evidently had read about the Taliesin Fellowship, a program for apprentices-in-residence that Wright and his third wife, Olgivanna, had launched the year before:

> I am writing to find out if you are at Spring Green now—I am coming to Chicago on Sunday [August 20] and am desirous of running up to Spring Green for a day to see what you are doing there. I saw a very meager report in a paper article of some work or project you are working out there. It caught my interest . . ..

Wright's quick response on August 21 made no effort to disguise his primary interest:

> We are at Spring Green and will be glad to have you with us. You will heartily approve of what we are trying to do, for it is after your own heart and salvaging under tremendous difficulties but with great encouragement what you and mother Lawrence helped along years and years and years ago . . . .
>
> If only a relic of the Lawrence fortune remains you should build a pretty cottage here on a hill over the water—take over a 300 acre farm here (priced at $12,000) with a mile of waterfront, and watch this enterprise grow, helping as you might with what talents and money you could spare and invest. Fate has been unkind to money.
>
> This is a beautiful corner of Earth. We are heading into a great work. We have everything but money but that lack can't last forever . . ..[15]

Wright may not have grasped the extent of her decline—or that of her house—until she wrote a long and painful letter on December 4, 1936:

> It is such a long time since I have been able to write any letters—after I last saw you all—and was so royally treated to your generous and appreciated hospitality.
>
> I suddenly stumped and came near going under completely. All the strain of the last 20 years came to a full culmination and got me. The responsibilities of business—changing conditions—family responsibilities—deaths of all members of my family.
>
> Strain of nursing my cousin, an inmate of my home ever since I was a small child. I never left her night or day during 6 and a half years but four weeks all days put together. She had disintegration of the spinal cord—agonizing suffering and sometimes 20 bad convulsions in 24 hours.
>
> I was the only one [that] could control them. When she passed I was left, as it were, a piece of human driftwood—and it has taken all this time to bring the cogs to catch again.
>
> Business on the West Coast had to have much attention, also here. I have been so crippled up all over my body I could hardly move . . ..
>
> I have always been more truly interested in the things you both were doing and working out than anything I have contacted so far.
>
> My own struggle to keep my head above water and work out my body and soul's salvation on some safe lines has taxed my courageous spirit, but I have conquered at last. Am still a long way from possessing the strength I hope to have.
>
> I had always given of strength, courage and what worldly possessions I had until now I am left with little in a material way to give, or even have for my needs, but I make no complaint. . . .
>
> My house here has been on the list of things I have not been able to look after and keep in constant repair—I could not take the necessary steps to look after it—I have always had a caretaker in it, and have been in the small house on the other side of the railroad . . ..

[14]After his trip to Japan in 1905, Wright foisted prints onto Walter Burley Griffin in lieu of salary. Griffin soon left the studio.

[15]Susan Lawrence later was listed among the "Friends of the Fellowship"; see John Sergeant, *Frank Lloyd Wright's Usonian Houses* (New York, 1976), p. 200.

> a time that there were only two houses I'd like to own in Springfield—and we now own both of them.[24]

Thomas planned to use the house as the new headquarters of his publishing firm, which had been at Third and Monroe Streets, only five blocks north. So he was used to the trains. He had the roof repaired with extra tiles discovered in the basement, had the masonry walls repointed, the copper gutters restored and the latticework rebuilt on the tall walls around the carriage house. He wrote Wright on February 8, 1944:

> Everytime I go to the house I find it is an inspiration. So do all members of my family. When we get into it we shall live and work there very quietly as it is like being in another world.

The publishing firm occupied the house in August 1944. Thomas installed what he described as a "huge new boiler" in the carriage house and built a tall chimney with bricks salvaged from the collapse of the north garden wall. The new heating system, he wrote Wright in 1945, kept the house at a remarkably even temperature during the winter months.

All this time, Miss Lawrence continued to live in St. John's Hospital. She could sometimes talk as lucidly as anyone, Earl Bice wrote Mrs. Anthony. About $70,000 remained in her estate, he said, and probably that would be enough unless she lived to be a hundred. She did not.

Susan Z. Lawrence died on February 20, 1946, at 83. She was survived only by a large number of cousins, all of whom lived out of town. The morning newspaper, from no apparent source other than hearsay, said she had inherited a fortune of $3 million and had spent $125,000 to build a house designed by Frank Lloyd Wright.[25]

In the spring of 1947, Thomas considered closing in the two verandas to expand the office space, but first he solicited the architect's opinion. Wright responded on May 5:

> Thanks—I should think that glass would be o.k. Better without it, but where you need it—why not?

His few words were enough to end the idea. Thomas did enclose the south porch, a change easily reversed in a later restoration of the house.

Thomas by 1950 had begun to plan a small book about the house to be written by Tom R. Cavanaugh, a graduate student at the University of Illinois, in Urbana. Wright agreed to review a draft of the text. In February 1951, Thomas asked for Wright's description of the significance of the window designs; he furnished Wright his own interpretations:

> 1) The top circle above the front entrance door is a band of butterflies.
>
> 2) The windows of the drawing room, east side, and the master bed room, directly above, at night when lighted up form a huge dragonfly. And that dragonfly runs in length from almost the floor of the bottom room to the top of the ceiling of the second floor.
>
> 3) The tall windows of the high room above the library are lilac tendrils.
>
> 4) The eight windows of the breakfast room are sumac bush designs.

Typically, instead of addressing the question, Wright responded on February 24 with a plea of his own:

> Can I ask a great favor. The Italian Exhibit of my life's work has no characteristic glass-work to show. Would you allow me to include the glass screen behind the fountain for the time of the foreign exhibition if I replaced it temporarily with plate glass. There are other specimens I would like but this is the finest of all . . .. I think there are five pairs of sash in the series—perhaps only four.
>
> We have stripped our Taliesin for the occasion and ask you to share our sacrifice. Due credit will be given you, of course.

Thomas soon explained his inability to satisfy Wright's sudden request:

> . . . [in 1946] my family formed The Thomas Foundation and into it was thrust bodily all of our property. Its terms and conditions are such that a Philadelphia lawyer might find it impenetrable, as one of its objectives was preserving the permanency

[24]Thomas' home was a brick Italianate villa with a three and a half-story tower, built in 1874–76 on Rte. 4 a few miles south of Springfield by Ben F. Caldwell, a farmer, banker and representative in Congress. "Inferior desecraters" was a favorite pun of Wright's. Thomas also reported in his first letter that the heating system would have to be replaced, the bowling alley was severely damaged, a set of andirons was missing, and the north court wall would have to be rebuilt. Four windows missing from the breakfast alcove were later recovered from an antique shop. Much of the latticework was gone from the top of the brick curtain walls around the carriage house; Thomas thought it had been of Louisiana cypress, but learned later that it was Wisconsin pine, rough-sawn, as was the exterior framing of the casement windows.

[25]*Illinois State Journal*, Feb. 21, 1946, p. 3.

> of this house, and keeping it in its integrity . . . for we know that some day the State of Illinois will want this treasure intact . . . and we shall try our best to keep it that way.

Wright fired off his answer on March 8:

> So that is how it is. The creative artist loses his right to his work for exhibition purposes so soon as it becomes "property."
>
> I have had occasion to curse the instinct and the system founded upon it before and now have the perfect example. I don't like to thank you for it but I guess I will have to.[26]

Thomas died in August 1968. He and his wife had saved the Dana house, but when the publishing firm left it early in 1981 the house again cried out to be rescued. A chain-link security fence now surrounded the front terraces. The plaster frieze had been stripped from the upper story. The pool in the garden court was gone. The bowling alley had been cut up into sections for table tops. The stained and scumbled sandfinish walls had been painted, and the red-oak trim had darkened almost to black.

The greatest threat, however, came from the art market. Collectors and museum curators, unembarrassed to regard fragments from Wright's buildings as mere objects of the decorative arts, were poised to pay exceedingly high prices for them. This meant that the house broken into bits and pieces could attain a far greater market value than the house kept intact.[27]

Thirty-five years earlier, Thomas and his wife meant to protect the house so it might someday become a cultural property of the state of Illinois; the early months of 1981 would test their vision. William G. Farrar of the state division of historic sites wrote the National Trust for Historic Preservation, in Washington, on March 23:

> Although the sale of the house would not normally indicate a danger, recent events have led me to believe that certain people are trying to acquire the property to sell off the furnishings and the windows . . . . I would hate to see this happen in Springfield.

On April 7, Charles L. Tamminga, associate director of the state bureau of lands and historic sites, wrote John A. Davidson, a state senator:

> The fact that the house is for sale at this time actually poses a danger to its preservation. Aside from the design quality of the house and its obvious real estate value, the fact that so much of the stained glass and sculpture exists coupled with the fact that the house also contains the largest intact collection of Frank Lloyd Wright furniture in the country makes it an obvious target for speculators. The million dollar asking price is cheap when one considers that the Bock fountain and the glass doors behind it could well go for a million dollars on the open market . . . . ownership by the State of Illinois would be an excellent way to preserve this example of our state's cultural heritage.

By happy coincidence, James R. Thompson was governor of Illinois and a collector of antiques. He appreciated the house as a rare work of art. A bill to appropriate $1 million to buy the house benefited from his strong support. It passed in the general assembly on June 30 and in the senate on July 29. A week later, the state took possession of the house; after 77 years it had become a public property.[28]

Only the year before, a professor at Greenville College, some 75 miles south of Springfield, had completed his dissertation at St. Louis University on the sculpture of Richard W. Bock. Donald P. Hallmark was also the director and curator of the Bock sculpture collection at Greenville College. He became site manager for the Dana house in October, and it was opened to the public on July 1, 1982.

After an exhaustive study of the historic structure, the Chicago firm of Hasbrouck Peterson Associates served as architects for the restoration. Wilbert R. Hasbrouck was the partner in charge. The aim was

[26]Wright's explosive reply is evidently the last time he wrote Thomas, who nevertheless continued to write politely, and sometimes with flattery, for six more years. Thomas had offered to send color pictures of the glass screen by Herbert Georg, an accomplished photographer. The deed from Thomas and his wife to the foundation is dated May 1, 1946; in September 1956 the title was conveyed to their son Payne E. L. Thomas and Wayne I. Bolinger of the publishing firm, and the foundation was dissolved the next month.

[27]The collecting of fragments was sanctioned and encouraged by the museum world, which can exist only by exhibiting items divorced from their original context and, usually, from their reason for being. Three windows from the Coonley Playhouse had entered the Metropolitan Museum of Art in New York as early as 1967. In 1972 an exhibition organized at Princeton University and titled "The Arts and Crafts Movement in America 1876–1916" included Wright's copper urn and copper weed holder, various chairs, art-glass windows and even an iron entrance gate from an apartment building. See my essay, "Dismembering Frank Lloyd Wright," *Design Quarterly* no. 155 (Spring 1992), pp. 2–5.

[28]At a reception in August 1991 at Wright's home and studio in Oak Park, Thompson said he was most often thanked for two accomplishments in his 14-year term as governor: "They say thank you for keeping the White Sox in Chicago, and thank you for the Dana-Thomas house"; see *Wright Angles*, vol. 17, no. 4 (Fall 1991), p. 1.

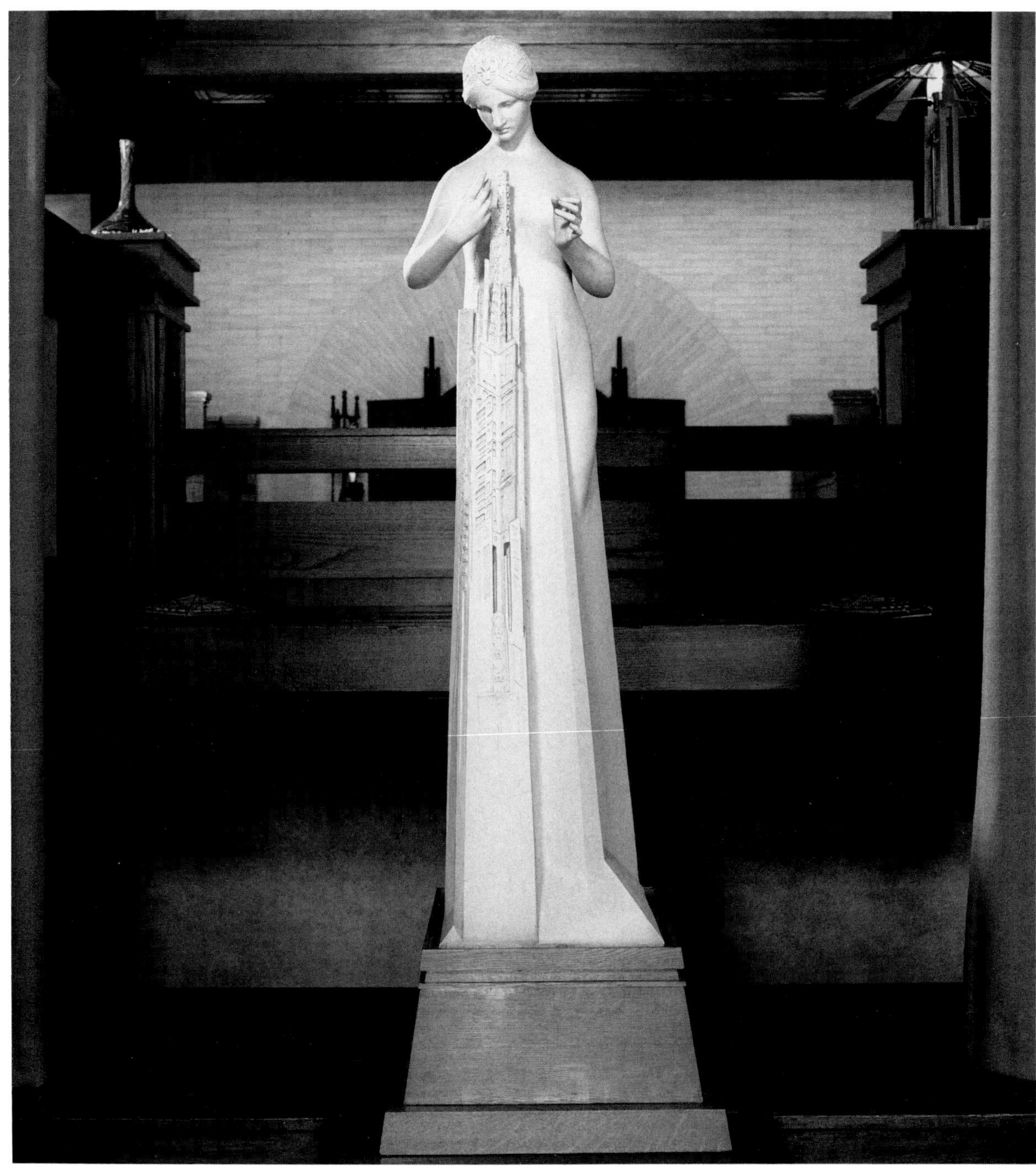

163. *"Flower in the Crannied Wall."*

to present the house as if in its prime, around 1910, when the landscaping was more mature, window screens and more lamps had been installed, the building fabric was gaining the patina of age, and Mrs. Dana was in her glory as a society hostess. The restoration proceeded meticulously and conscientiously. It took from September 1987 to July 1990. It included ancillary improvements and it cost the state $5 million.

A purpose of the Dana-Thomas House Foundation, incorporated in 1983, was to repatriate missing details. Fortunately, most of the furniture had failed to sell at the auction in 1943; but a few important objects, as well as three presentation drawings, had disappeared. Most of them began to come on the market. Governor Thompson acted through the foundation to raise major contributions from private sources, and more than $1 million was spent in 1987–88 to return various items to the house.

Philosophy begins in wonder, as the ancients said, but wonder can begin with art. The sculpture at the entry to the Dana house asks what architecture should be [163]. The answer comes from the house itself.

Index

(Page numbers in italics refer to illustrations only.)